Facing History and Ourselves:
Holocaust and Human Behavior
Annotated Bibliography

Edited by Margaret A. Drew

Walker and Company
New York

First published in the United States of America in 1988
by the Walker Publishing Company, Inc.

LIBRARY OF CONGRESS
Library of Congress Cataloging-in-Publication Data

Facing history and ourselves · holocaust and human behavior:
    annotated bibliography / edited by Margaret A. Drew.
        p.   cm.
    Includes index.
    ISBN 0-8027-9411-4
    1. Holocaust, Jewish (1939–1945)—Bibliography. 2. Holocaust,
Jewish (1939–1945)—Juvenile literature—Bibliography. 3. Genocide—
Bibliography. I. Drew, Margaret A. II. Title: Holocaust and
human behavior.
Z6374.H6F33   1988
[D804.3]
016.94053′15′039—dc19
                                                                88-21062
                                                                CIP

Contents

Facing History and Ourselves

Facing History and Ourselves is a non-profit organization providing educators with services and resources for examining the history of the Holocaust, genocide, racism, antisemitism, and issues related to adolescent and adult development. After attending workshops, individual teachers or an entire school district, may choose to use Facing History and Ourselves to enhance existing courses or as a complete program. The approach and methodology of the program have broad applicability for any study involved with difficult subject matter, multicultural education, critical thinking, and education about responsible citizenship.

The *Facing History and Ourselves: Holocaust and Human Behavior Annotated Bibliography* is part of a group of publications which includes:

1. a resource book: *Facing History and Ourselves: Holocaust and Human Behavior*
2. a companion manual to the Facing History videotape collection of survivor testimonies: *Facing History and Ourselves: Elements of Time*
3. a pilot resource book: *Facing History and Ourselves: Choosing to Participate*
4. a quarterly newsletter: *Facing History and Ourselves News*

Facing History educates about the failure of democracy in the Weimar Republic, the rise of Nazi totalitarianism and the genocide of the Jewish people of Europe during World War II. Students are encouraged to think critically about the role of individuals and groups in government, economics, social systems, and religion during the decades of choice before America entered World War II. They learn about the role of American presidents, individuals and institutions in bringing judgment to Nuremberg and the legacies this history has for education about the significance of citizen participation in preserving democracy, the rule of law and the opportunities for preventing abuses of human dignity and protecting human rights.

The program bridges the abstract ideas of history and ethics, and explores their application to society's problems today, making it useful in interdisciplinary ways. Facing History programs have been successful in facilitating a classroom and school environment which encourages participation. It engages students from mainstream and alternative programs in urban and rural environments and it helps them develop skills in reading, writing, and critical thinking. In addition, the program helps promote a sense of professionalism among educators at adopting sites and encourages educational leadership.

For further information about the activities, training or programs of Facing History, please write to Facing History and Ourselves, 25 Kennard Road, Brookline, MA 02146, or call (617) 232-1595.

Preface

There are a great many books about the Holocaust, and more are still being written. No individual can hope to read more than a fragment of the books available. Every bibliography must be selective, and each has its own unique perspective, even as each book does. The intention of this bibliography is to provide a wide range of reading for both students and teachers, including a variety of perspectives, both historical and literary. Each section of the bibliography consists of a selective list of books that represent a comprehensive, but not exhaustive, view of that aspect of the Holocaust.

The books included here represent an effort to explore the range of human responses to the Holocaust, as well as to provide the historical background necessary to place those responses in context. Some of the books are included because of the information they contain; others, because they represent a different way of looking at the Holocaust, either in content or literary style.

The compilation of this bibliography was a joint effort, and many individuals have contributed to it. From the inception of Facing History, suggestions have come from teachers, administrators, and friends, as well as from members of the Facing History staff.

Each book that adds another dimension or perspective makes its own unique contribution to the literature of the Holocaust, and to the understanding and awareness of the reader. Holocaust literature will certainly not be complete until the last survivor has written the last book; undoubtedly, not even then, as historians, literary critics, and the progeny of survivors continue to struggle with the unanswerable questions about the human condition which this piece of history demands that we address.

Editor
Margaret A. Drew

Children's Books

Children's Literature And The Holocaust

The Facing History resource book, **Facing History and Ourselves: Holocaust and Human Behavior**, contains a significant amount of reading material, however, in 400 pages it can only scratch the surface. Therefore, this bibliography is an attempt to guide readers to the vast amount of informaiton that is now available. These books do make an important contribution to the study of the Holocaust. Young people studying this period of history are frequently overwhelmed by the magnitude of the event. Six million Jews, 75% of the Jewish population of Europe, exterminated—the statistics defy imagination. It is difficult for the human mind to envision such statistics in terms of individual human beings. Films of the death camps, graphically depicting emaciated living skeletons and heaps of corpses, convey the inconceivable horror of the Holocaust, but tend to overwhelm and numb the mind. It is difficult to translate these scenes of atrocity into images of real human beings, once people like ourselves, going about their daily lives, holding onto their dreams, and coping with their disappointments.

This is where the reading of novels and personal accounts of Holocaust experiences can make a significant difference. These books can translate the statistics into people, can make historical truths accessible. The mind that cannot comprehend six million can identify with one person or one family, and then begin to expand that comprehension, as Andre Schwarz-Bart does in **The Last of the Just,** to "Ernie Levy, dead six million times," people now instead of numbers.

In order for literature to do this, however, consideration must be given, not only to what is read, but to when it is read. Most children have little knowledge of the Holocaust before they encounter it in the school curriculum; if the chief value of this literature is to make history accessible, then it is only logical that the history must come first. In addition, an individual book can only present a very small piece of the whole story; if it is the reader's only source of information, it is a distorted view of history. It is essential, then, that supplemental reading be exactly that—it should supplement, not substitute for, historical information.

Most books written for young people are about young people, and told through the eyes of the main character. Readers know no more than the protagonist knew, unless they bring that knowledge with them. A child hiding in an attic, or fleeing his or her homeland, did not understand what was happening, or why, or

how many others were also involved. Johanna Reiss's **The Upstairs Room** and
Hans Richter's **Friedrich** are good examples. The latter is an excellent portrayal of
two boys, one of whom is Jewish, growing up together in the early years of the
Third Reich; out of the context of history, it not only can distort reality, but
perpetuate stereotypes and misconceptions. **The Upstairs Room** is autobiographical; the author was ten years old when she and her older sister were hidden by a
Dutch family to escape the Nazis. It is an excellent book, effectively portraying the
experiences of these children and many others like them, but as a child's only
source of information about the Holocaust, it falls far short of the mark. For this
book to help a student understand the Holocaust, he or she must first have a place
in history to put it. Until children have enough historical background to provide a
context for what they are reading, they are reading stories, and nothing more.

After the background has been established, the question arises as to which
books students should read. Library shelves contain many stories written about this
period in history, many of excellent literary quality. In supplementing the history of
the Holocaust, however, it is necessary to distinguish between good literature and
good history. Some of these stories are glorious adventures of escape and resistance
that could, with a few minor changes, have taken place during any war, in any
country, at any time. Some of them, far too many, make absolutely no mention of
Jews; when they are mentioned at all, they are seen as passive recipients of the
generous aid provided by the heroes of the resistance. For example, history shows
that 85% of the Polish Jews were exterminated, yet most of the children's books set
in Poland at this time, except for recent titles like **The Cage** and **In the Mouth of
the Wolf,** are stories of resistance.

Little need be said about those books that are merely war stories; they
obviously contribute nothing to the study of the Holocaust. They may also be the
least harmful, as they are not seen as Holocaust books by the reader, and therefore
do not create distorted views in the reader's mind. They are harmful mainly to the
extent that they depict war as a glorious adventure. Presenting any war in that
manner is dangerous and irresponsible; romanticizing the story of the Third Reich
exhibits the same lack of integrity and moral responsibility that made the Holocaust
possible.

The escape and resistance stories present a more serious problem. Most
stories of the resistance are little more than adventure tales, glorifying and romanticizing war, creating marvelous heroes valiantly fighting to save their nation from
the Nazis. They leave a child thinking, "That must have been a wonderful, exciting
time—I wish I had been alive then." Resistance stories also present a distorted
definition of the word "resistance," a definition that implies only taking up arms
and meeting the enemy head-on. Sometimes it was overt physical resistance, as in

3

the uprising of the Warsaw Ghetto, but resistance was much more than that. Resistance was the performance of Verdi's Requiem in Terezin, it was keeping and burying records of personal experiences; to paraphrase one survivor, just to remain a Jew, in heart and mind, was in itself an act of resistance. There were many forms of resistance, and many heroes, few of whom bore arms; unfortunately, their stories have not been recorded in books for children.

The stories of escape and hiding present a more subtle problem. Read during or after studying the Holocaust, they can turn unimaginable horror into human experience; read in a vacuum, they convey little sense of what was happening outside the attics and upstairs rooms. Anne Frank's diary is the classic example: it is really much more a story of adolescence than of the Holocaust. Lawrence L. Langer, in his monumental work **The Age of Atrocity: Death in Modern Literature,** is referring to Gunther's **Death Be Not Proud** when he states, "For many, the book is to death what **Anne Frank: Diary of a Young Girl** is to the Holocaust. It circumspectly skirts the horror implicit in the theme but leaves the reader with the mournful if psychologically unburdened feeling that he has had a genuine encounter with inappropriate death." Miep Gies' recent book, **Anne Frank Remembered,** although not written for children, is not difficult, and puts the diary into historical perspective, as does the "Anne Frank in the World" exhibit currently touring the United States. Without this added insight, Anne's story, and many others like it, may lead readers to believe that they have had a "genuine encounter" with the Holocaust, when they have in fact only tiptoed around the edges.

The numerous other books available should be looked at carefully and used with discretion. It is not sufficient to judge such books according to literary standards alone; a book can pass all literary qualifications and still be badly out of step with history. In looking for appropriate books for young people, one should seek to stay within the limits set by Langer. In addition to the danger of failing to confront the issues, previously cited, Langer also warns against works that overemphasize the horrors; he refers to such works as "catalogues of atrocity" which, he states, "make dreary reading; a literature that failed to uncover traces of the human amidst the inhuman debris of our recent history would quickly lose its audience and might in fact be guilty of exploiting atrocity for questionable reasons." Children should be neither overprotected nor overwhelmed; although the aim is to enable young people to confront the Holocaust in a real and personal way, they should not be mired in despair. They can be informed without being paralyzed, with no room for hope.

Fiction

Forman, James   **Ceremonies of Innocence**
Hawthorn, 1970 (paper, Dell)
The leading characters of this novel are not fictional—Hans and Sophie Scholl really existed and were among the leaders of the student protest movement in Munich. They were executed for treason in 1943. Around them, and a number of their friends, Mr. Forman has woven a stirring novel, without the romanticism of many resistance stories.

Forman, James   **The Survivor**
Farrar, 1976
David Ullman is a Jewish Dutch boy, the son of a doctor who, in 1939, stubbornly refused to believe that Hitler's rise to power could have any effect on him. The novel follows the family through the war years: occupation, flight, capture, and the concentration camps. David is the only member of his family to survive Auschwitz and return to Holland, only to find his old home occupied by hostile, antisemitic strangers. His final pain is learning that, even though the Nazis have gone, the hatred still remains. This is a powerful novel, the only book thus far written for young people that truly expresses the horror of the Holocaust.

Gehrts, Barbara   **Don't Say a Word**
McElderry, 1986 (English translation; German edition, 1975)
An autobiographical novel of a young girl and her family living in a Berlin suburb, the story takes place between 1940 and 1943. Anna's father is an officer in the Luftwaffe, but is anti-Nazi; he is arrested and eventually executed. Anna's Jewish school friend and her family commit suicide. This is a revealing look at the German experience through the eyes of one who lived it. The author states in an afterword that she recorded her experiences after listening to young people in the late sixties who did not seem to understand the difference between freedom and tyranny.

Hartman, Evert   **War Without Friends**
Crown, 1982 (English translation; Dutch edition, 1975)
Arnold is a teen-age Dutch boy, whose father is a member of the Dutch National Socialist Party. Although Arnold is the only boy in the class who supports

5

the Nazis, and is subjected to the verbal and physical abuse of his classmates, he supports his father's position. Gradually, however, doubts begin to arise, even as his father's convictions move toward fanaticism. The father's convictions are a given, the basis for them never established, but the boy's position is stated with sensitivity and depth.

Innocenti, Robert   **Rose Blanche**
        Creative Education, 1985
    Although this has the appearance of a picture book, it is actually an art book, and not intended for the youngest readers. It is an artist's view of the Holocaust as seen through the eyes of a child, a girl called Rose Blanche (deliberately named for the White Rose resistance movement). It is also deliberate that the artist painted this picture story without a glimpse of the sky, thus adding to the feeling of oppression. The story attempts to transmit the child's lack of understanding of war, together with the child's refusal to believe or accept what she senses is happening around her. Innocenti says, "This book is meant to breed questions." An excellent book for use by either history or art teachers.

Ish-Kishor, S.   **A Boy of Old Prague**
        Pantheon, 1963
    At first glance, this title appears to have no direct relation to the Holocaust; it is a novel set in the Middle Ages. The story centers around a Gentile boy brought up to believe the Jews, confined to the Ghetto, are the property of the devil. His fear and horror when he is made bond-servant to an old Jew, and his growing respect and love for his master, make this excellent background, and help the younger reader understand the historical context of the Holocaust and the attitudes that made it possible.

Moskin, Marietta   **I Am Rosemarie**
        John Day, 1972 (paper, Scholastic)
    Rosemarie was a young Dutch Jew busily planning her summer vacation when the Germans invaded, and nothing was ever the same again. The persecution began mildly, with her expulsion from school, and ended in a concentration camp. This novel is more positive, perhaps less realistic, than Forman's **The Survivor**; Rosemarie's whole family survived the camps, and Rosemarie reached woman-hood, full of hope and promise. Read before the Forman book, this is inspiring; afterwards, it is an anti-climax. It is recommended for the student who might find the Forman book too harsh.

Orgel, Doris   **The Devil in Vienna**
        Dial, 1978
        This novel is a story of friendship between two girls, one Christian and one Jewish, the year that Hitler annexed Austria. Lieselotte has moved to Germany because of her father's Nazi sympathies, and Inge starts keeping a journal to help replace the loss of her friend. The book depicts the social and political climate of Vienna as it dramatizes the girls's struggle to maintain their friendship against enormous pressures.

Orlev, Uri   **The Island on Bird Street**
        Houghton-Mifflin, 1983
        The author of this novel, originally written in Hebrew, was born in Warsaw in 1931, and spent two years hiding in the Warsaw ghetto. In the novel, a 12-year-old boy hides for five months in an unnamed ghetto (not Warsaw). When Alex and his father are captured, Alex manages to escape; they had previously arranged to meet in a bombed-out house on Bird Street if one were captured. Alex demonstrates an ingenious talent for survival as he waits for his father's return. This is a realistic, well-written story of courage, hope, and loneliness.

Richter, Hans P.   **Friedrich**
        Holt, 1970 (paper, Dell)
        In his second novel for young people, **I Was There,** Hans Richter states that both of these books are autobiographical: "I am reporting how I lived through that time and what I saw - no more." In this first-person narrative, Friedrich is the friend and neighbor of the narrator; when the boys were born, in 1925, it mattered little that Friedrich was Jewish, and the two boys grew up together in friendship. By 1933, however, the persecution of the Jews had begun, and when the narrator's father joined the Party, it became a wedge separating the families. This simple, poignant story, aimed at younger readers and told from a child's perspective, dramatically describes the destruction of one Jewish family.

Samuels, Gertrude   **Mottele**
        Harper, 1976 (paper, New American Library)
        Like many other novels, this is fiction based on fact. Mottele is a 12-year-old boy who joins Uncle Misha's partisans, a Jewish resistance group, after his parents are killed by the Germans. In spite of his youth, he plays an active role in the resistance, and the book documents, in novel form, the activities of the partisans and the role Mottele played. A less comprehensive version of the same story, containing only Mottele's early days with the partisans, is **Uncle Misha's Partisans** by Yuri Suhl (Four Winds Press); the latter version is recommended for

younger readers. Documentation of the story, and excerpts from Uncle Misha's notes (his real name was Misha Gilderman), can be found in Suhl's **They Fought Back,** listed in the adult section of this bibliography.

Suhl, Yuri   **On the Other Side of the Gate**
         Watts, 1975 (paper, Avon)

This is the only novel for young people that is set in a ghetto; the main characters are a young married couple who chose to have a child after the Nazis had outlawed pregnancies in the ghetto. The baby was delivered in secret, and when plans for deportation were made known, was smuggled out of the ghetto to a sympathetic Polish family. In an afterword Mr. Suhl tells of the actual episode upon which he based this story. The novel is a moving affirmation of life in the midst of death, a declaration of the human will to live.

Personal Accounts

Bar Oni, Bryna   **The Vapor**
>Visual Impact, Inc., 1978

Bryna Bar Oni was 14 years old in 1939, when the Germans invaded Poland. Of the one thousand Jews living in her small Polish town, only 23 survived. Among the survivors were Bryna and one sister; the rest of her family perished. Now living in a Chicago suburb, Bryna writes of her "personal nightmare," describing her life with her family in the ghetto and their flight when they learn the ghetto has been scheduled for liquidation. After seeing the rest of their family killed, Bryna and her sister reach the forest partisans, where they remain until liberated by the Russian Army. This is a chilling account, recommended for older readers.

Isaacman, Clara (as told to Joan Adess Grossman)   **Clara's Story**
>Jewish Publication Society of America, 1984

Clara's family had left Romania for Belgium in the thirties; when Hitler invaded Belgium in 1940, they first tried unsuccessfully to escape to France, then to Britain. In 1942, the resistance placed them in hiding, with the exception of a brother who had gone to a labor camp. Her father was later killed, but the rest of the family survived by constantly moving from one "safe" house to another. This provides much more historical background than most stories of hiding, including in the family's story, reports about events outside their hiding places.

Koehn, Ilse   **Mischling, Second Degree**
>Greenwillow, 1977 (paper, Bantam)

Ilse Koehn was only six when the Nuremberg laws declared her to be a mischling, second degree, i.e., a person with one Jewish grandparent. She was not aware of her Jewish heritage, however; her story is simply that of a little German girl whose world seems to be crumbling for no understandable reason. The book chronicles her experiences, at home and in evacuation camps, from the thirties through to the end of the war.

Reiss, Johanna   **The Upstairs Room**
Crowell, 1972 (paper, Bantam)

By far the best of the stories that use the theme of escape or hiding, this is an autobiographical account of a 10-year-old Jewish Dutch girl. Along with her older sister, she is taken in by a Dutch family and hidden in an upstairs room of their farmhouse. A sequel, **The Journey Back** (Crowell, 1976), describes the aftermath of the war.

Sender, Ruth Minsky   **The Cage**
Macmillan, 1986

Riva Minska begins her story shortly before the German invasion of Poland in 1939, and dramatically describes the change in her non-Jewish neighbors. By 1942, then 16, she was guardian of her younger brothers in what had become the Lodz Ghetto; from there they move to Auschwitz. Her story is the most graphic found in children's literature, but is not overwhelming; her ultimate survival, as well as her spirit during her ordeal, place the emphasis on the power of the human spirit to overcome atrocity, rather than on the atrocity itself.

Siegel, Aranka   **Upon the Head of a Goat**
Farrar, 1981

The author is the girl named Piri in the story, nine years old at the beginning of the book, in 1939. She was Hungarian, but was visiting her grandmother in the Ukraine when the war broke out. It was over a year before she was able to return to Hungary, where she remained, first at home and then in the ghetto until deportation to Auschwitz in 1944. Her writing vividly conveys the struggle of a family to maintain hope and dignity in the face of separation, death, and the destruction of their whole way of life. Siegal's portrayal of her mother is especially strong. Her story is continued in **Grace in the Wilderness** (Farrar, 1985); opening just before the liberation, it is the story of her post-war years, with the time in the camps mentioned only occasionally in flashbacks.

von der Grun, Max   **Howl Like the Wolves**
Morrow, 1980

The author approaches his subject in a unique way, blending history with personal experiences. He was a German youth during the Holocaust, neither Jewish nor Nazi, and not directly involved in the war until 1944, when he was captured soon after joining the armed forces and sent to an American POW camp. The combination of history and memoir includes much original source material in the historical sections, while somewhat slowing down the narrative. It is an excellent presentation for the serious student.

von Staden, Wendelgard　**Darkness Over the Valley: Growing Up in Nazi Germany**
> Ticknor & Fields, 1981

　　As an adolescent girl, and the niece of Hitler's first foreign minister, the author was at first caught up in the National Socialist movement. Her mother was not, however, and gradually Wendelgard herself began to see the evil, especially after a Jewish labor camp was set up in the valley. In the end, she helped her mother provide aid and comfort to the Jewish prisoners; the mother is portrayed vividly as a brave, heroic woman, and the book provides new perspective on life in Nazi Germany.

Zar, Rose　**In the Mouth of the Wolf**
> Jewish Publication Society of America, 1983

　　Known as Ruska Guterman in her native Poland, Rose escaped from the Piotrkow ghetto and, traveling with false papers, held various jobs, once even returning to the ghetto to be with her father, the only other family member left. Eventually, she becomes housekeeper for an SS officer and his wife, following her father's advice that the safest place to be is "right in the mouth of the wolf." Her story is unusual, as few succeeded in surviving this way.

General Non-Fiction

Abells, Chana **Children We Remember**
    Greenwillow, 1986
    With a very sparse text, and graphic black-and-white photographs taken from the Yad Vashem collection, the author presents a striking glimpse of a life that has disappeared. As the title implies, the pictures are predominantly of children, beginning with pre-war scenes and progressing through the discriminations of the Nazi takeover, depicting resistance, but only touching the edge of the real horrors that these children endured.

Atkinson, Linda **In Kindling Flame: The Story of Hannah Senesh 1921-1944**
    Lothrop, 1985
    Hannah Senesh was a Hungarian Jew who emigrated to Palestine in 1939 and returned to Hungary during the war to try and rescue her people from the Germans. She was executed shortly before the Russians invaded Hungary. Atkinson has told Hannah's life story, smoothly interspersed with the relevant history of the times. The reader sees Hannah as a very real young girl and woman, with a great deal of insight into her inner thoughts and feelings, due to the diaries and poems that Hannah left. The story of Hannah's captivity before her execution comes largely from her mother, with some information from other prisoners. The history woven into this biography is essential for a full understanding of Hannah's life, and is readable and unobtrusive; the story of this courageous young woman is told with simplicity and sensitivity.

Bernbaum, Israel **My Brother's Keeper: The Holocaust Through the Eyes of an Artist**
    Putnam, 1985
    Bernbaum was born in Warsaw, and escaped as a young man just before the ghetto was established. He is now an artist in the United States, and has done a series of five highly symbolic paintings called "Warsaw Ghetto 1943," which he presents as a slide show in New York City schools. In the book, he reaches out to a larger audience, explaining the images and symbolism of each painting. On canvas, the paintings were large, and much of the detail is lost in the book, but the explanations and the use of cut-out sections of the pictures help point out things that the viewer might otherwise miss. Text and pictures dramatize and illuminate the heroes of the ghetto, as well as the all-too-few heroes outside the ghetto; he also depicts graphically the evil of the Nazis, and the callousness of the bystanders.

Finkelstein, Norman H.   **Remember Not to Forget: A Memory of the Holocaust**
>Watts, 1985

This factual book about the Holocaust is intended for the youngest readers, and illustrated with woodcuts. The history is related with simplicity, and with an honesty and lack of sentimentality rare in books on serious subjects for young children. Although the audience for this slim volume is much younger than any student using this curriculum, the book deserves attention here because it is the best, if not the only, book of its kind for young children. It is a book to be shared with the siblings, and parents, of students studying the Holocaust.

Friedman, Ina R.   **Escape or Die: True Stories of Young People Who Survived the Holocaust**
>Addison-Wesley, 1982

These personal stories chronologically portray the increasing intensity of danger and the diversity of the routes and destination taken by young people in order to escape the Nazis. To provide perspective, the author precedes each tale with a short history of the Jews in each country of persecution. Despite the fact that all the young people depicted here were survivors, the horrors of the Holocaust are not minimized, and the book does not become a series of exciting adventure stories, as do so many books of this type written for children. Fast reading for all ages.

Kluger, Ruth and Mann, Peggy   **The Secret Ship**
>Doubleday, 1978

An adaptation for young people of Kluger's earlier work **The Last Escape;** it is the true story of the illegal ship Hilda, which took hundreds of illegal Jewish immigrants from Rumania to Palestine. Ruth Kluger was in charge of organizing that operation. This is an easy to read and exciting story, but realistic and, at times, horrifying.

Meltzer, Milton   **Rescue: The Story of How Gentiles Saved Jews in the Holocaust**
>Harper, 1988

Meltzer has collected material from diaries, letters, eyewitness accounts, and personal interviews to document the stories of non-Jews who helped to prevent Jews from becoming victims of the Holocaust. These people came from throughout Nazi-occupied Europe, including Germany itself; they came from all walks of life, from countess to peasant, priest to policeman. In the midst of atrocity, they were the voices of hope and goodness, those who risked their lives to save others. This is an excellent supplement to Meltzer's **Never to Forget**, which details the history of Nazi destruction and Jewish resistance.

Noble, Iris   **Nazi Hunter, Simon Wiesenthal**
Messner, 1979
The first two chapters give a brief biography of Wiesenthal, describing his experiences under the Nazis—his mother's death in a concentration camp and his own narrow escape from a similar death on two separate occasions. The author describes Wiesenthal's start as a Nazi hunter, motivated originally by a desire for revenge. She then recounts his activities in searching out former SS men, including Adolf Eichmann.

Prague Museum   **. . . I Never Saw Another Butterfly**
McGraw-Hill, 1964
This is a collection of poems and drawings done by the children of Terezin Concentration Camp between 1942 and 1944. No one except a survivor can truly understand life in a concentration camp; however, one understands much more when looking through the eyes of a child. Students reading this book should first have had some background material about the camps; only then will they fully appreciate the hope and the fear that are expressed here. Only then, in the words of one of the poems, "Then if the tears obscure your way, / You'll know how wonderful it is to be alive."

Switzer, Ellen   **How Democracy Failed**
Atheneum, 1977
The author is a German Jew who emigrated to the United States in the 1930s, when she was a teenager. In the 1970s she returned to Germany to talk to Germans her own age about their memories of those years. The result is a combination of historical background and oral history. She also compares Germany and the United States, and talks with German teenagers of today about their perspective of those earlier years.

Ziemian, Joseph   **The Cigarette Sellers of Three Crosses Square**
Lerner, 1975 (paper, Avon)
The cigarette sellers were a group of Jewish children who survived in the Aryan section of Warsaw during the Nazi occupation, at the time of the Warsaw Ghetto and after its destruction. The author was a member of the Jewish underground who met and helped the children, and later recorded their amazing story. Some of the children were killed, but most of them are alive today; there are photographs of them as children and a group photograph taken with the author in 1970. The 1975 edition adds an epilogue which tells of the present lives of the survivors, and the death of the author in 1971.

History

Altshuler, David   **Hitler's War Against the Jews. A Young Reader's Version of The War Against the Jews 1933-1945 by Lucy S. Dawidowicz**
Behrman House, 1978
This retelling of Dawidowicz's work in most cases parallels the original; in some instances, one chapter has been broken down into two, and two chapters, on the Warsaw Ghetto and the Warsaw Uprising, have been added. The text has been simplified and abbreviated—the chapter on the camps, for example, is reduced from 25 pages to 4, but the information is presented clearly and concisely, supplemented by photographs. Other additions are margin captions and a section at the end of each chapter called "Issues and Values"; it includes an index and some historical documents.

Bernstein, Victor   **The Holocaust - Final Judgment**
Bobbs-Merrill, 1980
After an overview of those on trial at Nuremberg, the author, who was one of the journalists who covered the trial, reviews the history of Germany and the Holocaust through documents revealed at Nuremberg. Coverage extends from the collapse of the Weimar Republic to the concentration camps. He includes extracts from the Indictments and an index of documents. Originally published in 1947 under the title **Final Judgment.**

Berwick, Michael   **The Third Reich**
Putnam, 1971 (originally published in London by Wayland Publishers as part of the Documentary History Series)
This is probably the simplest of the history books, mainly because of its organization. The main topic of each section is printed in the margin, there is an appendix listing the table of events, and another with brief profiles of the main German characters. It is also indexed and illustrated with numerous photographs. The text is divided into six chapters: Hitler, the SS, the war, the Jews, the camps, and the Nuremberg trials.

Forman, James   **Nazism**
Watts, 1978
Mr. Forman attempts to answer two basic questions: who was Hitler, and what was Nazism? This is more concise than the Goldston book, listed later; the format, with frequent chapter subheadings, makes it easy to find specific information, even though the index is not as detailed as that in the Goldston book. It is a good companion to Goldston, as it is more objective but less detailed; both are organized chronologically, unlike the Berwick, which is arranged thematically.

Goldston, Robert   **The Life and Death of Nazi Germany**
  Bobbs-Merrill, 1967
  This is the most detailed account of the war itself in terms of military and political history. The first four chapters cover the birth and growth of the Nazi Party, followed by two chapters on the prelude to war. The remaining chapters chronicle the events of the war, ending with one brief chapter on the Nuremberg trials. It is very well indexed, and useful for verifying specific facts, especially with regard to Hitler and his General Staff.

Lidz, Richard   **Many Kinds of Courage: An Oral History of World War II**
  Putnam, 1980
  Lidz has recorded the personal experiences of individuals involved in various aspects of the war, from Berlin in the thirties and Poland during the occupation to the concentration camps and Hiroshima. Each segment opens with a historical note by the author.

Meltzer, Milton   **Never to Forget: The Jews of the Holocaust**
  Harper, 1976 (paper, Dell)
  Mr. Meltzer has written a definitive history of the Holocaust for young people, telling the story of the Jews rather than the story of the Nazis. The book is divided into three parts: History of Hatred, Destruction of the Jews, and Spirit of Resistance. It is both readable and well-documented, including a chronology and a lengthy bibliography. Teachers who desire historical background material less exhaustive than Dawidowicz's **War Against the Jews** or Levin's **The Holocaust** will find this source invaluable.

Patterson, Charles   **Anti-semitism: The Road to the Holocaust and Beyond**
  Walker, 1982
  Patterson begins with a description of antisemitism in ancient times and the Middle Ages, then goes on to discuss "emancipation" in Napoleonic France and reactions against it, antisemitism in Czarist Russia and the United States. Part II describes antisemitism in Germany from the end of World War I to the "final solution"; Part IV covers modern antisemitism, beginning with the Middle East, then the Soviet Union, the western world (Europe, Argentina, and Australia), and the United States. Material is factual, readable for junior high students.

Rogasky, Barbara   **Smoke and Ashes: The Story of the Holocaust**
Holiday, 1988
In addition to presenting a comprehensive history of the Holocaust in simple but dramatic prose, Ms. Rogasky responds to a number of frequently asked questions, from "Why did it happen?" to "Why didn't the Jews fight back?" She also includes chapters on the response of the United States and Great Britain and the uniqueness of the Holocaust. The text includes excerpts from original source material and is accompanied by maps and photographs. This complements and supplements, but does not duplicate Chaikim's **Nightmare in History.**

Rossell, Seymour   **The Holocaust**
Watts, 1981
The history and mechanics of prejudice are examined here; the author looks at prewar Germany and Hitler's rise to power. He studies the organization and implementation of the Holocaust, as well as its aftermath. There is a strong reliance on original source material. It includes two chapters on antisemitism, and chapters on the ghettos, Jewish resistance, and the war crimes trials. The reading is not difficult, and captions at the beginning of each section make it easy to use. Good index, short bibliography and source list.

Rubin, Arnold P.   **The Evil That Men Do: The Story of the Nazis**
Messner, 1977
This is history told in terms of good and evil, the choices men had to make all over the world. Much of the history is relayed through the words of survivors, or in case studies of actual people and the choices they made, for good or evil. There are separate chapters on the children, the role of the church, and the matter of guilt. Some segments are quite readable, although the book as a whole is not easy. There is a good bibliography and an index. Published in paper (Bantam) under the title **Hitler and the Nazis.**

Stadtler, Bea   **The Holocaust: A History of Courage and Resistance**
Behrman, 1973
This was the first book for young people about the Holocaust, and as the title indicates, the emphasis is on the resistance, in its many forms. The first two chapters are historical background, and there are three chapters about people who helped rescue the Jews, but basically this is the story of the Jews themselves--the ghettos, the camps, the women, the doctors, the press, the many people whose names are remembered for their courage. The reading level is the easiest of all the history books, and the style is informal and readable.

Young Adult Books

The books listed below were either written for, or are especially recommended for, older students. Full annotations for these titles are found in the sections of the adult bibliography indicated:

Fiction
Demetz   **The House on Prague Street**
Hayden   **Sunflower Forest**
Karmel-Wolfe   **Marek and Lisa**
Korschunow   **Night in Distant Motion**
Linn   **Book of Songs**
Lustig   **Darkness Casts No Shadows**
Ramati   **And the Violins Stopped Playing**
Spiegelman   **Maus**

Personal Accounts
Gies   **Anne Frank Remembered**
Glatstein   **Anthology of Holocaust Literature**
Gray   **For Those I Loved**
Gurdus   **Death Train**
Hart   **Return to Auschwitz**
Hersh   **Gizelle, Save the Children**
Jackson   **Elli: Coming of Age in the Holocaust**
Oberski   **Childhood**
Tec   **Dry Tears**
Wiesel   **Night**

Resistance
Flender   **Rescue in Denmark**
Scholl   **Students Against Tyranny**
Suhl   **They Fought Back**

Art, Literature, & Literary Criticism
Rhodes   **Propaganda**

History
Bauer   **History of the Holocaust**

Adult Books

History And Background

Allport, Gordon W.   **The Nature of Prejudice**
>Addison-Wesley, 1954 (abridged edition, Doubleday, paper)
>Although this is not specifically a Holocaust book, it is an important re-
source; looking at prejudice in depth provides greater understanding of the Holocaust and the people involved in it, both the victimizers and the bystanders. As
Professor Allport states, "without knowledge of the roots of hostility we cannot
hope to employ our intelligence effectively in controlling its destructiveness."

Bauer,Yehuda   **History of the Holocaust**
>Watts, 1982
>More than a history of the Holocaust itself, this volume explores the origins
of Nazism, and antisemitism, Jewish life and Jewish-German relations in the pre-
Holocaust years. Bauer also discusses resistance in a variety of forms, and details
events of the Holocaust years by country. Includes glossary, bibliography, and
index, and is suitable for high school and advanced junior high school students.

Bauer, Yehuda   **The Holocaust in Historical Perspective**
>U. of Washington Press, 1978
>Four essays dealing with issues of the Holocaust: the Holocaust and Ameri-
can Jewry; the use of such terms as holocaust and genocide, and the de-demoniza-
tion of Hitler; antisemitism in Europe and its relationship to the rescue of the Jews;
the "trucks for blood" blackmail attempt, and why it failed.

Bergman, Martin and Jucovy, Milton E., eds.   **Generations of the Holocaust**
>Basic Books, 1982
>The main focus of this report on psychoanalytic research is on the children of
survivors, but the survivors themselves, as well as the children of the persecutors,
are also dealt with in depth. Most of the contributors to the work are members of
the Group for the Psychoanalytic Study of the Effect of the Holocaust on the
Second Generation. This group undertook a study of the ways in which "trauma
inflicted upon victims of the Holocaust could be transmitted from one generation to
the next." It is a detailed, scholarly account, largely case studies of individual
analyses.

Braham, Randolph, ed.   **Perspectives on the Holocaust**
Holocaust Study Series (Kluwer-Nijhoff Publishing), 1983
As the title indicates, the eleven articles presented here provide a variety of perspectives on the Holocaust, and also attempt to put it in perspective. Part I contains five studies relating to the philosophical, psychological, and religious aspects; Part II includes historical and literary views, and concludes with a view through the eyes of a survivor, Jack Eisner. Alan Rosenberg's paper, "The Philosophical Implication of the Holocaust," is a well-done study of the paradoxes implicit in any philosophical look at the Holocaust.

Chorover, Stephan   **From Genesis to Genocide**
MIT Press, 1979
This history of the use of technology to control human behavior includes a chapter entitled "Genocide: The Apotheosis of Behavior Control." Here Chorover explores the evolution of the eugenics movement, the origins of Nazi racist theories in late 19th century Europe and America, and the way these theories merged with social, political, and cultural conditions in the Germany of the thirties.

Dawidowicz, Lucy   **The War Against the Jews, 1933-1945**
Holt, 1975 (paper, Bantam)
The author, in her introduction, asks the persistent question about the Holocaust—"How could it have happened"— but she says that this question really embraces three separate questions: "1. How was it possible for a modern state to carry out the systematic murder of a whole people for no reason other than that they were Jews? 2. How was it possible for a whole people to allow itself to be destroyed? 3. How was it possible for the world to stand by without halting this destruction?" Her book is an attempt to answer these three questions; some reviewers have called it a definitive work of history.

Fein, Helen   **Accounting for Genocide: Victims—and Survivors—of the Holocaust**
Free Press, 1979
Ms. Fein views genocide from two viewpoints: a historical, or what she refers to as "macroscopic" view, and the victims' view. She begins with a look at the Armenian genocide, and then surveys the Holocaust as to national differences in Jewish victimization, church responses, the role of allied governments, the Judenrat, and social defense movements. She then describes the victims' view in various countries, through personal accounts. The book includes lengthy notes and bibliography; it is an important and insightful work.

Feingold, Henry L.   **The Politics of Rescue**
Rutgers University Press, 1970 (paper, Schocken)
The sub-title of this work is **The Roosevelt Administration and the Holocaust, 1938-1945.** In the preface, the author states that he "attempts to move beyond the moral aspect to examine the political context in which America's response was conceived." He discusses and evaluates various attempts to resettle European Jews, efforts to change refugee policies, and the roadblocks to rescue attempts.

Fleischner, Eva   **Auschwitz: Beginning of a New Era?**
KTAV, 1974
This anthology contains the papers of an International Symposium held in 1974 at the Cathedral Church of St. John the Divine in New York, where leading Jewish and Christian scholars from a wide range of disciplines -- sociology, philosophy, theology, psychology, history, and literature -- confronted the meaning of Auschwitz. The opening paper, by Irving Greenberg, clarified the central purpose of the symposium: "... both religions have continued since 1945 as if nothing had happened to change their central understanding. It is increasingly obvious that this is impossible, that the Holocaust cannot be ignored."

Friedlander, Henry and Milton, Sybil, eds.   **The Holocaust: Ideology, Bureaucracy, and Genocide. The San Jose Papers**
Kraus International Publications, 1980
This volume contains most of the papers presented at the two conferences held by scholars in San Jose, California, in 1977 and 1978. The first conference was concerned with the "significance of the Holocaust in fairly general terms"; the second focused more specifically on "the role of the educated elite and the professions in the Third Reich and Nazi-occupied Europe." Contributors include the editors themselves, in addition to Raul Hilberg, Henry Feingold, Lawrence L. Langer, and numerous others. The volume is divided into six sections, each dealing with a different aspect of the Holocaust.

Friedman, Philip   **Roads to Extinction: Essays on the Holocaust**
Jewish Publication Society of America, 1980
Philip Friedman has been called "the father of Holocaust history"; he was a Polish Jew, himself a survivor, and a historian of Polish Jewry prior to the Holocaust. From the end of the war until his death in 1960, he devoted himself to scholarly research on the Holocaust. This volume is a collection of his major essays. It includes an essay on the extermination of the Gypsies and several on various aspects of Holocaust research. The appendix gives an outline of a program for Holocaust research designed by Friedman in 1945.

Adult Books

Gilbert, Martin   **Atlas of the Holocaust**
Steimalsky's Agency Ltd., 1982
Combining geography and history, the maps appear chronologically, beginning with anti-Jewish violence in Europe between 1918 and 1932, tracing geographically the destruction of European Jewry, and ending with the post-war killing and flight of survivors up to 1950. The text is interwoven with the maps, supplementing the visual history.

Gilbert, Martin   **The Holocaust: A History of the Jews of Europe During the Second World War**
Holt, Rinehart & Winston, 1985   Paperback, 1987
After a brief historical account of antisemitism, Gilbert traces the history of the Holocaust from 1933 on. His account is based on a combination of historical research and personal accounts of survivors. The book contains over 800 pages of text, with an additional 60 pages of notes and sources, and another 60 pages of index. It is a very readable history, and includes many excerpts from the testimony of survivors. The result of years of Holocaust research, this is a definitive history for all who wish to know more about this painful period of history.

Hilberg, Raul   **The Destruction of the European Jews**
Holmes & Meier expanded edition, 1983 (3 vols.)
The author states in his preface that this is not the story of the victim, but of the perpetrator. In almost 800 pages of fine print, he explores the destruction process and details "the vast organization of the Nazi machinery of destruction"—expropriation, concentration, mobile killing operation, deportations, and killing center operations.

Hartman, Geoffrey, ed.   **Bitburg in Moral and Political Perspective**
University Press, 1986
This is a wide ranging and comprehensive group of essays on the moral and political implications of the Bitburg Affair. It includes an introductory survey by Saul Friedlander on the "new revisionism" among German historians and a fascinating never before published analysis of moral dilemmas generated by the Holocaust written by the distinguished sociologist, Theodore W. Adorno.

Hilberg, Raul, ed.   **Documents of Destruction**
New Viewpoints, 1971
Original source material is presented here, consisting of papers by "German perpetrators or Jewish victims." Most of the German material is made up of official documents; the Jewish sources are primarily autobiographical accounts. It provides an important supplement to his other work, listed above.

Hoffmann, Peter   **German Resistance to Hitler**
Harvard University Press, 1988
The book is divided into two parts, the rise of Hitler, which offers nothing new in the familiar story, and the Resistance, which concentrates almost entirely on two well known instances of military opposition, the 1938 controversy with General Ludwig Beck, which led to the General's resignation as Chief of the General Staff, and the July 20, 1944 assassination attempt; civilian opposition, such as the White Rose and the Kreisaw Group, is mentioned only in passing. Hoffmann makes the point that the German Resistance, unlike those of German-occupied Europe, received no encouragement from the allies and could not look for respect from their fellow countrymen. Such opposition as did exist, despite savage repression and the general acceptance of a Nazi regime, was often poorly organized and unrealistic in its goals.

Horowitz, Irving   **Taking Lives: Genocide and State Power**
Third edition. Transaction Books, 1980
The author, a professor of sociology and political science at Rutgers, has done a scholarly study of genocide. He describes it as "a singular type of mass murder, a historically distinct event that had its ultimate expression in the Holocaust." He also states, however, that "the fate of the Armenians is the essential prototype of genocide in the twentieth century." In addition to these examples, he discusses collectivism in the USSR, terrorism, and foreign policy with regard to human rights.

Korman, Gerd, ed.   **Hunter and Hunted: Human History of the Holocaust**
Viking, 1973
This is a chronological history, from the refugee crisis in the thirties to the liberation, assembled from contemporary documents and personal testimony. Selections include excerpts from Chaim Kaplan's diary, Elie Wiesel, and Raul Hilberg, as well as many lesser-known writers. Some of the material is available elsewhere, but the perspective provided by the organization of this volume makes it unique.

Lanzmann, Claude   **Shoah: An Oral History of the Holocaust**
Pantheon, 1985
The complete text of Claude Lanzmann's 9-1/2 hour film is presented here. Because of the length of the film, the text is a useful guide; although there is no index, the format of the book makes it relatively simple to locate specific interviews, which could then be used directly from the text, or in conjunction with the film.

Laqueur, Walter   **The Terrible Secret: Suppression of the Truth About Hitler's "Final Solution"**
>   Little Brown, 1980

In this volume, Professor Laqueur addresses three basic questions: when did information about the exterminations become known; through what channels was the information transmitted; and what was the reaction of those who received the information? He tries to discern whether the truth was deliberately suppressed or simply not believed, covering only the period from June, 1941 to December, 1942. The emphasis is not on why nothing was done, or whether anything could have been done, but only on who knew, and who believed, seeking answers to the "wider cognitive questions: what is the meaning of 'to know' and 'to believe'?"

Levin, Nora   **The Holocaust: The Destruction of European Jewry, 1933-1945**
>   T.Y. Crowell, 1968 (paper, Schocken)

The first part of this historical account moves chronologically, detailing the Nazi program for the Jews and demonstrating its implementation. The second half is divided by countries, and illustrates how the Nazi program was affected by individual governments and degrees of antisemitism. She emphasizes the resistance of the Jews, rejecting the statements of others regarding their passivity, and discusses the rescuers and the bystanders from other parts of the world, including the United States.

Morse, Arthur D.   **While Six Million Died: A Chronicle of American Apathy**
>   Hart, 1967 (paper)

In his introduction, the author states, "If genocide is to be prevented in the future, we must understand how it happened in the past—not only in terms of the killers and the killed but of the bystanders." Much of the literature of this period echoes the statement that the Holocaust could not have happened if the world had not stood by and let it happen—that it did not happen in Denmark is a case in point. Morse documents what was and was not done by the American government from 1933 to the end of the war, quoting extensively from official documents.

Pisar, Samuel   **Of Blood and Hope**
>   Little Brown, 1979

This is a combination of personal teestimony from a survivor with commentary on the political and economic situation today. According to the author, the book is an attempt to integrate the realities of the past with the problems of the present; he believes that "economic integration could replace political confrontation," that increased economic ties between East and West is the only way of "defending humanity from the risk of self- destruction." It is a controversial book which, according to Dorothy Rabinowitz, proves only that "that can never be made to seem other than what it is, even clothed in the authority of the Holocaust."

Whether the reader agrees with Pisar or Rabinowitz, the book is thought-provoking.

Poliakov, Leon   **Harvest of Hate: The Nazi Program for the Destruction of the Jews of Europe**
> Greenwood Press, 1954   (paper, Schocken)
> One of the earliest histories of the Holocaust, this book was reissued in 1971. As the sub-title indicates, it is less a history of the Holocaust per se than a history of the Nazi program, from **Mein Kampf** to the death camps. There are sections on the "industry of death," Nazi programs for "inferior people" other than Jews, and reactions and attitudes among the European people. It is well-documented, with much original source material.

Rubenstein, Richard L.   **The Cunning of History: The Holocaust and the American Future**
> Harper, 1975 (paper, Harper)
> This brief volume is an attempt to put the Holocaust into historical perspective; the author places the Holocaust on a continuum that begins in Judeo-Christian tradition, continues to slavery, and culminates in twentieth-century bureaucracy. It is not really a book about the Holocaust, but rather a re-interpretation of the meaning of Auschwitz. Rubenstein's thesis is sometimes controversial, but nevertheless thought-provoking and interesting.

Sachar, Abram L.   **The Course of Our Times: The Men and Events That Shaped the Twentieth Century**
> Knopf, 1972
> Sachar, Chancellor of Brandeis University, begins this overview just before the First World War, and concludes with Communist China up to 1971. Students of the Holocaust will find his chapter on Hitler and Nazism of value, but one of the most important chapters is called "The Reaction of the West to Genocide," which deals with both the Holocaust and the Armenian genocide. Sachar concludes in this chapter, "Part of the tragic toll must be attributed to bystanders, righteous bystanders, safe in the fellowship of virtuous platitudes that make the whole world kin . . ."

Sherwin, Byron L. and Ament, Susan G., eds.   **Encountering the Holocaust: An Interdisciplinary Survey**
> Impact Press, 1979
> This compilation of scholarly studies on various aspects of the Holocaust was designed for the purpose of "developing a model interdisciplinary curriculum in Holocaust studies for American colleges and universities." Part One deals with the historical, political, and psychological aspects; Part Two, with the art of the Holocaust; Part Three, with theology and philosophy. Each article includes a

Adult Books

bibliography. Sherwin himself wrote several of the essays; other contributors include Arnost Lustig and Helen Fein.

Sichrovsky, Peter   **Born Guilty: Children of Nazi Families**
Basic Books, 1988
The Austrian journalist Sichrovsky investigates how children (and grandchildren) of former Nazi war criminals deal with their heritage. Leading questions that Sichrovsky posed in interviewing these children were: What did they really know of their parents activities, and how did they find out? When did their vague suspicion harden into knowledge of what their parents had been involved with during the war? In light of the current scholarship among certain right wing German historians who seek to minimize the importance of the Nazi experience in German history, it is telling to learn of contemporary German youth, especially those who are descendants of Nazis, who are attempting to confront the past and understand the significance of the Nazi legacy in their country's history.

Trunk, Isaiah   **Judenrat**
Stein & Day, 1977
The ruling Jewish bodies in the ghettos of Eastern Europe were the Jewish Councils, the Judenräte. Trunk has provided an objective, well-researched history of the Councils—external and internal factors, conditions under which they performed, their motivations and actions, and the results of their activities. He uses both archival documents and eyewitness reports, and addresses the question of collaboration on the part of the Councils.

Wiesenthal, Simon   **Sunflower**
Schocken, 1976
The first part of this volume is a story—the story of a young German soldier who, from a hospital bed, recounts to a young Jewish camp survivor the atrocities he has participated in. To alleviate his guilt, he asks forgiveness from the Jew, but receives only silence. The second part of the book is a symposium of responses to the Jew's silence, and the issue of forgiveness, by prominent theologians and philosophers.

Wyman, David S.   **Abandonment of the Jews: America and the Holocaust 1941-1945**
Pantheon, 1984
What did America know about the extermination of the Jews, who knew, and when did they know? These are the questions Wyman addresses as he traces the role of the State Department and the Roosevelt administration, revealing the failures of the United States to respond to the desperate needs of European Jews.

Fiction

Appelfeld, Aharon   **Badenheim 1939**
> David R. Godine, 1980
>
> This short, Chekhovian novel is set in a resort town near Vienna, where a group of cultured Jewish vacationers are spending the spring of 1939. Although never explicit, impending doom seems to be always on the edge of the reader's mind, perhaps only because the hindsight of history makes the date meaningful to the reader in a way that would not have been understood at the time. Irving Howe, in a New York Times review, said, "Trivial events follow trivial events to the very edge of the Holocaust, before which Mr. Appelfeld stops abruptly, as if to recognize a limit to the sovereignty of words."

Appelfeld, Aharon   **Tzili: The Story of a Life**
> Dutton, 1983.
>
> Tzili, a young Jewish girl, is the subject of neglect and ridicule, because she is considered "simple-minded"; with the onset of war, she is left to fend for herself, while her family flees. Her wanderings and sufferings can serve as a metaphor for all Jews during this time.

Demetz, Hana   **The House on Prague Street**
> St. Martin's Press, 1980
>
> Prague, before and during the war, is the setting for this quiet story of a teen-age Czech girl who falls in love with a German soldier. In a low-keyed but powerful novel, the author shows in very personal terms the intrusion of destruction and terror into the tranquil life of a middle class Jewish family. In terms of making the reader understand what the victims felt, one reviewer says this book comes "as close as art can, to making the terrible truth universally accessible."

Gary, Romain   **The Dance of Genghis Cohn**
> World, 1968
>
> This French novel is set in 1968; Genghis Cohn is a Jewish comic who had been shot by a German firing squad more than twenty years earlier, but has returned as the dybbuk of a former SS official. Schultz, the SS officer, is currently investigating the murders of 22 male victims; the perpetrators of these deeds turn out to be symbols of Humanity and Death. The tragicomedy is rich in humor and symbolism, called in Der Spiegel, "Faust revived by the Marx brothers."

Note: There are also works of fiction included in other subject areas.

Hayden, Torey   **Sunflower Forest**
Putnam, 1984

Lesley is a 17-year-old girl in Kansas, whose life differs from other girls only in that her mother seems exceptionally vulnerable, and has spells where she becomes excessively emotional and depressed. At first, Lesley knows only that her mother came from Germany, and had some unpleasant experiences during the war. Gradually, she learns that her mother was taken as part of a Lebensborn experiment, where she gave birth to two baby boys. The first was taken from her; the second, she smothered; now, many years later, she is convinced that a local child is her lost son. There are no simplistic solutions here: the ending for the mother is tragic; for Lesley, after much searching for understanding, only confusion and an awareness of the complexity of the problem. A well-written, moving novel—not for those who seek easy answers and neat endings.

Karmel-Wolfe, Henia   **Marek and Lisa.**
Dodd-Mead, 1984

This novel about two young people, their separation and reunion, begins as Lisa wakes up in a hospital. She has been freed from a concentration camp as the war is winding down, but shot for snatching a vegetable from the ground. The story of her romance and marriage is told in flashbacks, as doctors strive to heal her leg. Marek's story begins about midway through the book, as he begins his search for Lisa. There is one especially revealing scene where Lisa, recovering in a German hospital, looks out her window into the apartment of a German family, and asks, "Where are all the terrible Germans?" Her question is answered by a Jewish friend and benefactor: ". . . every place . . ." This is a well-written, moving young adult novel.

Korschunow, Irina   **Night in Distant Motion**
David R. Godine, 1983

Regine, a 17-year-old German girl, is a loyal Nazi until she falls in love with a Polish prisoner, a "subhuman." Her feeling for Jan makes her begin to question Nazi doctrine and become aware of what is happening in Germany. She and Jan are caught together; she is captured, escapes, and is hidden by a farm family. The story is told in flashbacks, while she is hiding in the farmhouse; the whole story of her relationship with Jan and her capture is not revealed until the book is almost over. This novel paints a revealing portrait of the ways in which the German people were deluded by Nazism; Regine's parents felt that Hitler "made life worth living again for us Germans." "We owe it all to the Führer!" was their constant refrain. The relationship between Regine and Jan is intimate, but not graphically portrayed; the book is suitable for mature junior high readers.

Kosinski, Jerzy   **The Painted Bird**
Houghton Mifflin, 1965 (paper, Bantam)
A description on the cover of the paperback edition calls this the story of a "young boy escaping the Holocaust through war-torn Europe"; this sounds like so many other books that it leaves the reader completely unprepared for the nightmare that unfolds. The intense brutality and graphic descriptions of extreme cruelty are almost unbearable; it is the only book that ever literally gave this reviewer nightmares. Yet, as Lawrence L. Langer has stated, this work demonstrates the lowest point of inhumanity that mankind is capable of, and until we have faced this horror, we have not truly confronted the Holocaust.

Laqueur, Walter   **The Missing Years**
Little Brown, 1980
Laqueur's first novel probably has more value as history than as literature; this is not surprising, as he is best known as a historian. The novel does, however, provide an interesting perspective on the war years, as its protagonist and narrator is a Jew who remains in Berlin throughout the Nazi era.

Linn, Merritt   **A Book of Songs**
St. Martin's Press, 1982
The setting for this allegorical novel is a work camp, where many of the inmates are former musicians. The narrator describes the workers in the factory as the orchestra, with the supervisor as the conductor. Wandering through the camp is a small boy who plays the violin in return for scraps of food. The narrator finds purpose in living by devoting himself to looking after and eventually freeing the boy. There are many memorable characters here, and although suffering is not minimized, the book emphasizes hope and ends with liberation (although the boy and the narrator are the only survivors). Because this is a long book, with much philosophy and introspection, only mature high school readers will appreciate it, but for them, it is a gem.

Lustig, Arnost   **Darkness Casts No Shadows**
Inscape, 1976 (paper, Avon)
A summary of the plot could easily make this sound like typical "escape fiction." Rather than emphasizing the excitement of escape, however, the author painstakingly describes the moment-by-moment struggles of two young boys and the bitter memories that haunt them as they make a desperate stab at freedom. They have escaped from a transport, leaving a concentration camp, and probably on route to a death camp. They are trying to find their way "home," though only the reader seems to realize that such a place probably no longer exists.

Ramati, Alexander   **And the Violins Stopped Playing**
                     Watts, 1986
Ramati based his novel on notes given to him by Roman Mirga, the main
character in the story, so although written as a novel, it is actually a personal
account of Mirga's experience as a Polish Gypsy from 1942 to 1945. Mirga was in
his teens at the time, the son of the man who led the tribe out of Poland only to fall
into the hands of the Nazis as they invaded Hungary. They are sent to Auschwitz,
where Roman is assigned to assist Dr. Mengele. His story, as told by Ramati,
presents a vivid picture of Gypsy life, and a devastating view of the Gypsy holocaust.

Schwarz-Bart, Andre   **The Last of the Just**
                       Atheneum, 1960 (paper, Bantam)
The cover of the paperback edition describes this as "the epic novel of the
Jewish experience," and that is not an exaggeration. Based on the traditional Jewish
legend of the 36 just men, the author traces the Levy family from Rabbi Yom Tov
Levy in the Middle Ages to young Ernie Levy, who perished at Auschwitz, the last
of the just. This book does for adults what **A Boy of Old Prague** does for children,
and more; it chronicles 800 years of Jewish history in the story of one family. So it
was for millions; in the author's words, "I can't help thinking that Ernie Levy, dead
six million times, is still alive somewhere."

Spiegelman, Art   **Maus: A Survivor's Tale**
                   Pantheon, 1986
Spiegelman is a cartoonist who uses the medium at which he excels to tell
the story of his father, a survivor of Auschwitz. In this volume, the Jews are mice
and the Nazis are cats, but the events are both human and inhuman. The depiction
of Nazi Germany as a gigantic mousetrap only adds to the power of the image.
Spiegelman takes his parents to the gates of Auschwitz, planning a second volume
to conclude their story. This is a unique and powerful perspective on the Holocaust,
necessitating a new definition of the term "comic book."

Thomas, D.M.   **The White Hotel**
                Viking, 1981
This strange but powerful novel combines Freudian psychoanalysis, sexual
fantasy, poetry, and prose with the horror of the Holocaust to create a graphic and
dramatic portrait of a woman's search for personal fulfillment. Twenty years after
the opening of the story, the case study, along with the poetry and the fantasy,
come to an abrupt end in a ravine at Babi Yar. The author refers to the "terrain" of
this beautifully written novel as "the land of hysteria." This may be the first
attempt to merge Freudian thinking with the Holocaust; the confrontation is almost
overwhelming.

Tournier, Michel   **The Ogre**
> Doubleday, 1972 (paper, Dell)

A prize-winning French novel, this has been described as a "magnificent fairy tale." In a skillful blend of history and myth, the author relates the bizarre odyssey of a French garage mechanic turned soldier who is captured by the Germans and becomes, in an ironic turn of events, chief assistant at a Nazi military school. The book is rich in symbolism; it is an allegory linked with the legends of St. Christopher, the Erl King, and ultimately, the Apocalypse. It is a literary masterpiece, a revelation of profound truths and pathological perversions of truth.

Traub, Barbara Fischman   **The Matruska Doll**
> Richard Marek, 1979

This marvelous novel concerns a Jewish girl in Transylvania. The story opens with her liberation from Auschwitz, then goes back to her earlier years; it then picks up the original thread and continues through the Russian liberation and the Communist takeover, with occasional flashbacks to childhood and Auschwitz. In the end, as Lisa Engles is fleeing her country to escape from Communism, she says, in the book's closing words, "I knew I had survived but I was not sure I was free."

Personal Accounts

Day, Ingeborg　**Ghost Waltz: A Memoir**
Viking, 1980
　　Now an American, this Austrian-born woman confronts her past and her prejudices when, after her father's death, she searches into his Nazi past. She learned when she was seventeen, and a student in the United States, about Germany's role in World War II and the Holocaust; she knew her father fought in that war, but when she returned home and tried to talk to him about it, he refused to discuss it. Her reflections, recorded here, combine with historical research and personal soul-searching in an effort to understand both her father and herself. This is a unique point of view, and a moving portrait of an individual who was, in her own way, also a victim and a survivor.

Djilas, Milovan　**Wartime**
Harcourt Brace Jovanovich, 1977
　　Djilas was a Vice-President of Yugoslavia until his expulsion and imprisonment in 1954, and one of Tito's three top aides. This is his third autobiographical work, and concerns mainly the Partisan warfare in Yugoslavia and the Communist rise to power. It includes many personal recollections of Tito, as well as descriptions of partisan battles, and discussion of major issues in Partisan warfare, such as whether or not you continue to fight if one hundred of your countrymen will be killed for each dead German.

Donat, Alexander　**The Holocaust Kingdom: A Memoir**
Holocaust Library (Schocken), 1978
　　Donat was a Polish Jew who, with his wife and son, survived the Warsaw Ghetto and Maidenek death camp. At Maidenek, he was separated from his family and sent to a labor camp, and then to Dachau, where he remained until liberation. He was reunited with his wife and son, and they emigrated to the United States in 1946. Along with his personal story are many memorable vignettes of people and events whose paths he crossed; the final section is his wife's account of the time between their separation and their reunion.

Note: There are also personal accounts under other subject headings.

Fenelon, Fania **Playing for Time**
Atheneum, 1977
The author was a member of the women's orchestra in Auschwitz from January 1944 to liberation. Her book provides revealing descriptions of this aspect of life in the camp—the interpersonal relations and reactions, and the behavior of the female Kapos. CBS-TV has done a two-hour docudrama, adapted from the book and carrying the same title (of which Miss Fenelon did not approve), and also a 16 minute film called **Music of Auschwitz**, originally produced as a segment of "60 Minutes."

Glatstein, Jacob, ed. **Anthology of Holocaust Literature**
Atheneum, 1968 (paper)
The selections in this anthology were translated from several languages, and attempt to show the scope and diversity of Holocaust literature. Almost all the selections were written by witnesses to the events they describe. There are sections on the ghetto, the concentration camp, and the resistance, among others. This is an excellent source of personal accounts; most of the selections are only a few pages long, and could be used with students.

Gray, Martin (with Max Gallo) **For Those I Loved**
Little Brown, 1972 (paper, NAL)
Martin Gray was 14 when the Germans invaded Poland, and so traumatic were the experiences of the war that he remembers almost nothing of his life before that. After the invasion, he became a member of the Jewish Resistance in the Warsaw Ghetto; later he was a soldier in the Russian Army, then a secret police officer in Russia, and by the age of 35, a well-to-do American businessman. His experiences with tragedy and death were not over, however, as the ending of the book reveals. This is an intense, powerful account of one man's struggle for survival, a fascinating and compelling autobiography. There is also a brief photographic essay by David Douglas Duncan called **The Fragile Miracle of Martin Gray** (Abbeville Press, 1979).

Gurdus, Luba Krugman **The Death Train**
Holocaust Library (Schocken), 1978
The author, a Polish Jew, begins her story with the birth of her son in 1938. After the German invasion, her husband and brothers join the armed forces, and the rest of the family, including her parents and sister, begin shuttling from place to place in a desperate attempt to survive. She loses her son and her parents, is sent to a concentration camp, but survives to find both her sister and her husband after the liberation. Original drawings illustrate this book and add much to a warm, personal account.

Adult Books

Hart, Kitty   **Return to Auschwitz**
Atheneum, 1981
After making her TV documentary in 1978, Kitty Hart has put her entire life story into book form. She begins by describing her arrival in England—a moving picture of a 19- year-old girl, who survived Auschwitz, holding on "in the assurance that there *had* to be light at the end of the tunnel. And still there was no light . . . even in the outside world there are so many different ways of beating people to their knees." She backtracks to describe her life before Auschwitz, the process that eventually ended in Auschwitz, and the return. Her story is told simply and movingly, in a personal way that makes it easy for readers to visualize and participate in her experiences.

Hersh, Gizelle and Mann, Peggy   **"Gizelle, Save the Children"**
Everest House, 1980
This story of a family of Hungarian Jews was co-written by the oldest daughter. She was sixteen when their ordeal began, and the title stems from her mother's last words to her, as they were separated at Auschwitz. It was these words that kept Gizelle going when giving up frequently seemed easier. Faithful to her mother's charge, she brought her three sisters through, though neither her brother nor her parents survived. This is written in conversational style, the narrative flows smoothly, and it is a good choice for young people.

Hillesum, Etty   **An Interrupted Life: The Diaries of Etty Hillesum**
Pantheon, 1983
Etty's journals cover the years from 1941 to 1943; she was 27 when they begin, a well-to-do, highly assimilated Dutch Jew. The early stages of the diaries are intimate accounts of her personal life, and gradually become more concerned with outside events, as her own awareness and involvement grows. Terrence Des Pres calls this book "a marvelous gift."

Jackson, Livia E. Bitton   **Elli: Coming of Age in the Holocaust**
Times Books, 1980
Elli was 13 in 1944, when her village was invaded; along with her brother, her parents, and her aunt, she was transported to Auschwitz. She and her mother remained together throughout, and twice made contact with her brother. From Auschwitz they were taken to work in a German factory, then to Dachau. The autobiography presents a detailed account of life in the camps, from the perspective of an adolescent—at times describing unimaginable horrors, at others concern with her appearance, a young man, or a new dress. It is a moving portrait of a stolen youth, an adolescent **Survival in Auschwitz.**

34

Kuznetsov, Anatoli, (A. Anatoli)   **Babi Yar: A Document in the Form of a Novel**
Farrar, Straus & Giroux, 1970 (revised and uncensored edition)
paper, Washington Square Press
The author lived in Kiev, not far from the ravine known as Babi Yar; in
this volume he recalls his childhood, from the German invasion of Kiev to its
recapture by the Russians. It is a very personal story, but it also contains many
descriptions of people and events, including eyewitness accounts of the atrocities
committed at Babi Yar. It is important to read the 1970 edition; the book was
previously published in 1966, in a direct translation of the censored Russian
version. The 1970 edition was published after the author defected; it has the previously censored material in bold-faced type, and new material in brackets. The
paperback edition is uncensored, but has a uniform type face.

Leitner, Isabella   **Fragments of Isabella: A Memoir of Auschwitz**
Crowell, 1978
The author was a Hungarian Jew, born Isabella Katz, one of six children;
she was in her teens when the transport left for Auschwitz with her whole family
aboard except her father, who was in America trying to obtain immigration papers
for the others. Her brief but intensely moving story is more a memorial than a
memoir; a memorial to her mother, who left such a legacy of love and hope and
faith in the ultimate triumph of humanity over inhumanity that her children were
able to find the strength and the determination to survive. This slim volume is a
monument to the human spirit.

Leitner, Isabella   **Saving the Fragments: From Auschwitz to New York**
New American Library, 1985
The continuation of Mrs. Leitner's story opens with the Russian liberation
and chronicles her journey, with her two surviving sisters, to the United States,
where they are reunited with their father. They arrived on the day that the war in
Europe ended, thus being the first survivors of the camps to reach the United
States. Hers is a story more of feelings than facts. In exquisite prose, she reveals
her thoughts and feelings as she struggles to cleanse herself of the death and hatred
of Auschwitz and reestablish her links with humanity. This is a worthy successor to
her earlier book.

Oberski, Jona   **Childhood**
Doubleday, 1983
This short, simple autobiography of a young Dutch boy (only seven when
the war ends) is told in the first person, and reflects only what the child himself
sees and understands. He and his mother are captured and then released; later, the
entire family is taken, and both the parents are killed. Conversations are reported as
the child heard them, but the reader understands more than the child did. This view

of the Holocaust from the mind of a small child is devastating in its simplicity and understatement.

Tec, Nechama   **Dry Tears: The Story of a Lost Childhood**
Oxford, 1982, 1984 (paper)
This first-person narrative is by a woman who is now associate professor of sociology at the University of Connecticut; she was eight years old when the Germans invaded her native Poland. She and her family survived by living with other families on the Aryan side. She presents this ordeal through a child's eyes, but with the added knowledge and perspective of the adult. Even though they escaped the worst horrors of the Holocaust, her detailed accounts of daily life bring home to the reader the feelings of a young child who witnessed killings in the streets and was selling on the black market at the age of 12. The epilogue (only in the 1984 edition) describes the author's post-war experiences.

Wiesel, Elie   **Night**
Hill & Wang, 1960 (paper, Avon)
Elie Wiesel is probably the best known of all writers on the Holocaust. He was born in Hungary in 1928; he and his family were deported to the concentration camps, where his parents and younger sister died. **Night** was his first book; it is a memoir of those experiences, the story of a teenage boy caught in a nightmare. Because of the author's masterful style and imagery, it reads like a novel, but conveys more reality than history. In **The Holocaust and the Literary Imagination,** Langer says that this slim volume "drew this portion of history into the unlimited aspirations of literary art, and gave it a resonance and universality which only imaginative literature could achieve."

Wolf, Christa   **Model Childhood**
Farrar, Straus & Giroux, 1980 (Paperback: **Pattern of Childhood**)
The author is an East German novelist; in this memoir she describes a visit to her native town, now a part of Poland. She took the trip in 1971, accompanied by her husband and 14-year-old daughter. Ms. Wolf was four years old when Hitler invaded Poland, and her family had been supporters of Hitler. The narrative jumps back and forth between past and present in a manner that is sometimes confusing, but her descriptions of her family and the local townspeople provide insight into the Germans who believed in Hitler.

Non-Jewish Victims

It is important to be aware of the fact that the Jews were not the only victims of Hitler's persecution. Gypsies, Poles, and other Slavic people were also considered "inferior"; many were imprisoned and killed, and many more were slated for extermination. Although these victims are mentioned in some of the books listed in other sections of this bibliography, those listed below have been singled out as having particular importance in this area and to draw attention to this frequently overlooked aspect of the Holocaust. Several of the books were published in Poland and deal specifically with the victimization of the Polish people, both Jewish and non-Jewish. The Polish Embassy is to be thanked for providing those materials, and Gloria Grzebien and Jean Babiec of the Rhode Island Heritage Commission for their assistance in locating material on this subject. *

Auschwitz: Nazi Extermination Camp
Warsaw: Interpress, 1978
This book is written in five sections, each by a different author. The sections are: a historic outline, including the genesis of the camp; the prisoners; extermination; resistance; and lastly, the prosecution of the criminals. It is a readable and informative account, available in five languages.

Bialoszewski, Miron   **A Memoir of the Warsaw Uprising**
Ardis, 1977
The author has been described as one of Poland's leading post-war poets. He was 22 when the uprising began in August of 1944. The rebellion itself failed, but the city held out for two months before the resistance was finally destroyed. This memoir does not give a military history or tell tales of heroic martyrdom; rather, it depicts the daily life of an ordinary citizen, a view of the uprising as seen from the ruins and sewers in which he hid. It was written 25 years after the event, and according to the translator's introduction, was considered by some to be a "blasphemous mockery" when first published in Poland.

Boczek, Helena, and others   **Wojna i Dziecko**
Warsaw: Nasza Ksiegarnia, 1979
The best English translation of the title is "War and the Child"; it is a pictorial account of the war as it affected children. The preface and captions are printed in six languages. It is a graphic, chilling visual account of children in wartime.

* For further information, contact:
Polish Embassy, 2640 16th Street, NW, Washington, DC 20009
Rhode Island Heritage Commission, Old State House, 150 Benefit Street, Providence, RI 02903

Adult Books

Hancock, Ian   **The Pariah Syndrome: An Account of Gypsy Slavery and Persecution**
Karoma Publishers, Inc., 1987
This is an overview of the history of Gypsies from their origins until the present. The chapter on Gypsy history during the Third Reich emphasizes that the Nazi oppression of Gypsies represented a continuation of discriminatory policies against Gypsies that had been practiced since the Middle Ages. A comprehensive bibliography is included.

Hillel, Marc and Henry, Clarissa   **Of Pure Blood**
McGraw-Hill, 1976 (paper, Pocket Books)
There has been little information in the extensive literature of the Holocaust about the Lebensborn, Hitler's plan to breed a master race. The authors spent three years collecting the material in this book, and much of the information presented here has been documented for the first time. They discuss the breeding farms and the kidnapping of thousands of non-German children who possessed the right physical characteristics for Germany's breeding stock. They also document the results of these attempts to breed a master race: the number of backward children in these homes was 15% above average. This work provides horrifying proof that Nazism did not treat humanely even the people it considered superior.

Kulski, Julian Eugeniusz   **Dying, We Live: The Personal Chronicle of a Young Freedom Fighter in Warsaw (1939-1945)**
Holt, 1979
Kulski was the Protestant son of the Mayor of Warsaw; he was ten when the Germans invaded Poland. In spite of his youth, he became a freedom fighter in the Polish Resistance, witnessed the uprising of the Ghetto, was jailed by the Gestapo, and taken prisoner of war. His account was written shortly after the war, as he recorded his experiences in journal form.

Pilichowski, Czeslaw   **No Time Limit for These Crimes**
Warsaw: Interpress, 1980
This is a history of the Nazi policies and practices in Poland. It includes the Nazi treatment of POWs, children, and women, and has separate chapters on slave labor, detention centers, ghettos, and camps. Much of the source material for this book came from the Polish Archives.

Plant, Ian   **The Pink Triangle: The Nazi War Against Homosexuals**
Henry Holt and Company, 1986
This is the first comprehensive study available in English on the treatment of homosexuals in Nazi Germany. Plant examines the ideological motivations for the persecution of homosexuals and traces the actions of the Third Reich to carry out policies for purifying the Aryan race of the "poulting stranger." This is an important work for examining the relationship between Nazi ideology and Nazi policies.

Yoors, Jan   **Crossing: A Journal of Survival and Resistance in World War II**
Simon & Schuster, 1971
The son of a Flemish artist, Yoors ran off with a Gypsy family when he was twelve; he spent several summers thereafter with the Gypsies and winters at home with his parents. When war broke out, he persuaded his Gypsy "family" to help form a group to work with the resistance, while he served as intermediary. He describes these resistance activities and his own later efforts to smuggle refugees into Spain; in addition, he creates a vivid portrait of his Gypsy family and their way of life.

The Ghettos

Becker, Jurek **Jacob the Liar**
Harcourt Brace Jovanovich, 1975 (English edition; original edition, 1969)
Jacob's story is set in a Polish ghetto toward the end of the war; Jacob accidentally hears a German radio broadcast news report of Soviet army advances when he is sent to the police station for curfew violations. In order to pass on the information without admitting to having been taken to the police station, he tells his friends that he has a hidden radio. The ramifications of this lie seem to be endless, and when he finally confesses the lie to a friend, the friend commits suicide—the "radio" had given people cause for hope. A marvelous novel of irony, tragedy, hope, and despair, written by a man who spent most of his youth in the Lodz ghetto and in concentration camps.

Cholawski, Shalom   **Soldiers From the Ghetto: The First Uprising Against the Nazis**
A.S. Barnes, 1980
The first uprising took place in the ghetto of Nesvizh, Poland, in July of 1942, when the Nesvizh Jews burned their ghetto to the ground, fought the Nazi invaders, and fled into the forests. There they formed a partisan army that went on, joined by other partisans, to harass the German forces as they moved toward Moscow. The author was commander of that band of ghetto partisans, and has provided a first-hand account of their activities in a stirring portrayal of a little-known piece of Holocaust history.

Czerniakow, Adam   **The Warsaw Diary of Adam Czerniakow** Edited by Raul Hilberg, Stanislaw Staron, & Josef Kermisz
Stein & Day, 1979
First published in Hebrew in 1968, the diary itself begins in 1939, when Czerniakow was the appointed Chairman of the Jewish Council and Warsaw was invaded by Germany. The diary, consisting of several notebooks, was given to Yad Vashem by a ghetto survivor in 1959. Czerniakow, as head of the Council, was the instrument through which the Nazis gave orders for deportations, and finally took

---

* There are a number of novels about the ghettos, such as John Hersey's **The Wall**, Leon Uris' **Mila 18**, and more recently, Leslie Epstein's **King of the Jews**; in addition, Arnost Lustig's **Night and Hope** is a fine collection of short stories set in the Theresienstadt concentration camp not far from Prague. In the interest of space, however, and because of the wealth of original source material and eyewitness accounts, primarily non-fiction works have been listed here.

his own life rather than continue to serve in this role. The diary gives historical information and records the day-to-day problems of a Jewish bureaucrat trying to function under intolerable circumstances. He is a controversial figure in history, regarded by some as a martyr and by others as almost a collaborator.

Dobroszycki, Lucjan, editor   **Chronicle of the Lodz Ghetto, 1941-1944**
Yale University Press, 1984
The men who kept the records of events in the Lodz Ghetto were determined that the world should know what happened there; they worked both collectively and officially, as the Department of Archives, and recorded everything from weather reports to deportations. The editor of this volume was a survivor of the Lodz ghetto, and is now a researcher at the YIVO Institute; he is eminently qualified to provide the introduction and analysis of these excerpts. The excerpts themselves present a vivid and disturbing picture, particularly with regard to its leader, Mordecai Chaim Rumkowski (the basis of Epsteins's novel, **King of the Jews**), and perhaps raise more questions than they answer. The documents are similar in kind to those that chronicle the Warsaw Ghetto, but they differ as Lodz differed from other ghettos, and paint a devastating portrait, what Elie Wiesel calls "multifaceted agony."

Eisner, Jack   **The Survivor**
Morrow, 1980
Jack Eisner was 13 when the Nazis defeated Poland; he became part of a gang that smuggled food and arms over the wall into the Warsaw Ghetto. His story continues through the uprising to the camps, escape, recapture, and finally liberation. This book reveals the anger and violence of the ghetto teenagers who would today be called "street kids," equivalent in lifestyles, attitude and behavior to the urban ghetto youths described in books like Piri Thomas' **Down These Mean Streets**. Although there is both sex and violence in this book, high school students may find the raw emotions revealed here make ghetto life real in a way not accomplished by any history book.

Grossman, Mendel   **With a Camera in the Ghetto**
Schocken, 1977
Only one Jewish photographer succeeded in getting a camera into a ghetto—the ghetto was Lodz, Poland, and the photographer was Mendel Grossman. The pictures delineate the lives of the people during the years 1941 and 1942. The text includes the first English translation of portions of **The Chronicle of the Lodz Ghetto**. For many, the visual impact of a photograph is more effective than thousands of words; for them this book will convey all the agony of the Holocaust.

41

Hyams, Joseph   **A Field of Buttercups**
            Prentice-Hall, 1968
        The story of Janusz Korczak, born Henryk Goldszmidt, has been recon-
structed from his diary, and from conversations with many who knew him, located
by the author in Europe, Israel, and the United States. Most of the book concerns
the orphanage that Dr. Korczak ran in the Warsaw Ghetto, but it also touches on his
earlier life, and on other ghetto activities. Hyams describes the march of Dr.
Korczak and his orphans to the railway station for deportation, and the later
uprising and destruction of the ghetto itself.

Kaplan, Chaim   **The Warsaw Diary of Chaim A. Kaplan**   Translated and
edited by Abraham Katsh
            Collier, 1973 (paper)
        Originally published in English in 1965 under the title **Scroll of Agony**,
this edition includes entries that were not available then. Kaplan was a scholar,
educator, and a habitual diarist, 59 years old when the Nazis invaded Poland. This
portion of his diaries, from September 1, 1939 to August 4, 1942 (his final entry),
were among others smuggled out of the ghetto before its destruction. The member
of the Polish underground who received them later gave some of them to Professor
Ber Mark and brought others to the United States when he emigrated in 1962.
These were sold to the editor of this book and made up the text of the first edition;
Katsh later discovered missing entries at the Jewish Historical Institute in Warsaw,
and added them to the new edition. Kaplan himself is believed to have died at
Treblinka in late 1942 or early 1943.

Korczak, Janusz   **Ghetto Diary**
            Holocaust Library (Schocken), 1978
        The first part of this volume is a prose poem called "The Last Walk of
Janusz Korczak" by Aaron Zeitlin, a noted Yiddish poet. It is followed, after an
explanatory preface, by Korczak's diary, which is not an outline of his activities
but a reflection of his thoughts and feelings. This gives an introspective view of
the well-known Polish martyr who went to his death rather than abandon his
orphans. Hyams' **A Field of Buttercups**, listed above, is a narrative of events, and
gives more factual information about the doctor's life.

Kurzman, Dan   **The Bravest Battle**
            Putnam, 1976 (paper, Pinnacle)
        This is a detailed daily account of the uprising of the Warsaw Ghetto, put
together from original documents and interviews. One reviewer states that this
research helps point out "the moral ambiguity that results when people are caught
in extreme situations." It further shows that people caught in hopeless situations
can sometimes respond with valor instead of despair.

Mark, Ber   **The Uprising in the Warsaw Ghetto**
Schocken, 1975 (paper)
Professor Ber Mark was a renowned historical scholar and one of the founders of the Jewish Historical Institute in Warsaw. In the first half of this volume he reconstructs the uprising from its beginning on April 19, 1943 through August, 1944, when the last known individuals were still living in underground caves in the ghetto. Part II is made up of documents related to the uprising—reports from the underground and other Jewish organizations, as well as documents from the German and Polish governments.

Meed, Vladka   **On Both Sides of the Wall: Memoirs From the Warsaw Ghetto**
Hakibbutz Hameuchad Publishing House, 1977 (paper, Schocken)
Although the first English edition of this did not appear until 1973, the original Yiddish edition was published in 1948, making it the "first authentic document about the uprising and destruction of the Warsaw ghetto, as well as about the Holocaust in general," as Elie Wiesel states in the introduction. Ms. Meed's memoirs begin in 1942, when the first deportation order was issued in the ghetto. She joined the underground, smuggling weapons in and people out, and because of her Aryan appearance was thus able to witness events from "both sides of the wall."

Ringelblum, Emmanuel   **Notes From the Warsaw Ghetto: The Journal of Emmanuel Ringelblum**
McGraw-Hill, 1958 (paper, Schocken)
Ringelblum was the archivist of the Warsaw Ghetto, 39 years old at the time of the invasion and already a promising historian and author. As a social historian, he saw the importance of collecting documentary materials; with a trained staff, he accumulated information and kept detailed personal notes until he was smuggled out of the ghetto, just before the uprising in 1943. He was executed in 1944, but the archives and notes had been buried under the ruins of the ghetto, in two separate sections. The first section was located in 1946; the second, including his personal notes, was uncovered in 1950.

The Camps

Améry, Jean   **At the Mind's Limits: Contemplations by a Survivor on Auschwitz and its Realities**
Indiana University, 1980
In the first of five essays, the author states that his purpose is "to talk about the confrontation of Auschwitz and intellect," the intellectual or cultivated man in Auschwitz. In the essay called "Torture," for example, he discusses the experience of torture, its effect on the victim, and the nature of the torturer. The book was first published in 1966 and reissued with an additional preface in 1977; the author committed suicide in 1978.

Auschwitz Album   Text by Peter Hellman
Random House, 1981
Lili Jacob Meier, an inmate of Auschwitz, collapsed as the American liberators arrived, and was carried into a vacated SS barracks. Here she discovered this album of Auschwitz photographs, and recognized the first picture as that of her own rabbi. Copies were made available to the Jewish Museum in Prague in 1946, but Lili carried the album around with her until 1980, when she presented it to Yad Vashem. Lili's story is told as a preamble to the photographs, 188 of them, accompanied by brief explanations. These are the only photographs ever taken of the process from the arrival of the trains to the killing facilities.

Bettelheim, Bruno   **The Informed Heart**
Free Press, 1960 (paper, Avon)
The subtitle of this book is **Autonomy in a Mass Age**; Dr. Bettelheim explores many aspects of human behavior in modern mass society, especially in extreme situations. He was an inmate of Dachau and Buchenwald from 1938 to 1939, when he was released and made his way to America before the war. He writes about his experiences and observations there, particularly about the passivity of the prisoners. This is a detailed, scholarly work, and the material on the concentration camps is only a portion of the book; readers may prefer an excerpt which appears in **Out of the Whirlwind: A Reader of Holocaust Literature**, by Albert Friedlander, listed in another section of this bibliography.

Bor, Josef   **The Terezin Requiem**
Knopf, 1963 (paper, Avon)
This is the inspiring story of Raphael Schächter, a young orchestra conductor imprisoned in the Terezin concentration camp. Schächter was determined to perform Verdi's Requiem at the camp, feeling that it captured both the fate and the hope of his people. Battling against disease, death, and transport trains, he struggled to assemble his musicians; he finally succeeded in performing the

Requiem, not only for his fellow prisoners but before a Nazi audience that included Adolf Eichmann. Bor's story of this remarkable man is brief and movingly written as a tribute to Schäcter and the other artists of Terezin by one who was himself a survivor of that camp.

Borowski, Tadeusz   **This Way to the Gas, Ladies and Gentlemen**
Viking, 1967 (paper, Penguin)
Borowski was born in the Ukraine, but moved with his family to Warsaw when he was 10. At 20, he published his first volume of poetry, through an underground press in Nazi-occupied Warsaw. He was arrested and spent two years in Auschwitz and Dachau. After the liberation, he began writing again; his best works, from which these stories are taken, were published in 1948. In 1951, at the age of 29, he committed suicide. He is one of the few writers to get into the minds of the participants in and witnesses to the atrocities committed in the camps. He writes, not of events and experiences, but of morality, of what people did in order to survive. These remarkable, powerful, and painful stories lend understanding to the issues of corruption, apathy, and above all to the hope that led the victim to take his few remaining possessions with him to the gas chamber.

Delbo, Charlotte   **None Of Us Will Return**
Beacon, 1968
The author is French, a survivor; this volume is the first of a tetralogy, but the only one thus far published in English. She describes her experiences in a way that take the reader not only inside Auschwitz, but inside the prisoner herself. Her poetic prose and visual images are unsurpassed in Holocaust literature. Among many unforgettable passages is the one on thirst, ending, "When there is a bitter taste in the mouth, it means one has not lost the sense of taste . . ." Langer, who discusses her work in depth in **The Age of Atrocity**, says this "harshly poetic, despairingly beautiful vision . . . is a tribute to the power of the imagination to evoke the inexpressible."

Des Pres, Terrence   **The Survivor: An Anatomy of Life in the Death Camps**
Oxford, 1976 (paper, Pocket Books)
Des Pres has made an extensive search through the literature of the survivor, investigating the capacity of men and women to maintain their humanity in times of extremity. His questions are "addressed not to the fact that so many died, but to the fact that some survived." He says that he is not interested in the concentration camps themselves, "but rather with the people who suffered those places . . . an experience such as theirs cannot be understood apart from its context." Both Des Pres' approach and his conclusions differ radically from Bettelheim's.

Frankl, Viktor   **Man's Search for Meaning**
Beacon, 1959 (paper, Simon & Schuster)
The book is subtitled "an introduction to logotherapy," which is the
author's term for existential analysis. Dr. Frankl is a psychiatrist who was a
prisoner in a concentration camp, and his theories are based on his own experiences. Part 1 of the book, which makes up more than half its total length, is entitled
"Experiences in a Concentration Camp." He does not intend to describe life in the
camps, but rather how that life was reflected in the mind of the prisoner. He
discusses apathy, humor, curiosity, and hope, for example, in order to explain why
and how people maintain the will to live in such unlivable circumstances.

Garlinski, Josef   **Fighting Auschwitz**
Fawcett, 1975 (paper)
This is a well-documented account of the underground movement in
Auschwitz. Over half the book centers around Witold Pilecki, a Pole who went
voluntarily into the camp to organize a resistance movement. Though there was no
general uprising in Auschwitz, there were numerous escapes and much underground activity, including successful plots against some of the camp officials.

Kielar, Wieslaw   **Anus Mundi**
Times Books, 1980
Kielar was among the first to be imprisoned in Auschwitz, arriving on
June 14, 1940, the date of the camp's official opening. Although he says little about
his own background, Garlinski's **Fighting Auschwitz**, listed above, identifies him
as one of a group of Polish resistance fighters. Kielar remained at Auschwitz until
liberation; he describes the events, atmosphere, and effects of camp life in graphic
and brutal terms. The book won two awards when first published in Poland in 1972.

Langer, Lawrence L.   **Versions of Survival: The Holocaust and the Human
Spirit**
State University of New York Press, 1981
Langer investigates and assesses theories of survival as put forth by such
writers as Bettelheim, Frankl, and Des Pres, then analyzes material that contradicts
those theories. He goes on to look at the work of Elie Wiesel, and evaluate it in
terms of Wiesel's version of survival. In the final chapter, he examines language
itself, "as it succumbs to atrocity and then is reshaped into a new and vigorous if
enigmatic force by the hand and imagination of the poet." Langer challenges the
concept that there is a prototypical survivor, or any simple theory of survival that
can be adequate.

Levi, Primo   **Survival in Auschwitz**
Orion Press, 1959 (paper, Collier)
Primo Levi was an Italian Jew, captured in December of 1943; he was among those still at Auschwitz when the Russian liberators arrived. He provides documentary evidence of the life at Auschwitz, in terms of both outward activities and inner reactions. He speaks of the destruction of the personality, which he sees as more dangerous than the physical discomfort and the desperate aloneness in the struggle to survive. One of the most interesting sections of his story is the description of life in the camp just before the liberation, when the guards and all the relatively healthy prisoners were gone, and only those not capable of traveling were left.

Pawelczynska, Anna   **Values and Violence in Auschwitz: A Sociological Analysis**
University of California Press, 1979 (paper)
The author, a Polish sociologist and a survivor of Auschwitz, begins with a brief account of the camp in its historical setting and physical appearance. She then describes the ways in which the Nazis attempted to reach their main objective, "the biological destruction of prisoners," and the ways in which the prisoners resisted. She discusses the effect of differences in social background on survival, and the inner and outer resources that made survival possible. It is both readable and insightful, frequently contradicting Bettelheim's theories.

Selzer, Michael   **Deliverance Day: The Last Hours at Dachau**
Lippincott, 1978
Selzer has recreated the last day at Dachau from the points of view of several different people—American soldiers, prisoners, a German soldier, and the sole survivor of a transport train—in a moving and exciting account that reads almost like a novel. He concludes with current information about the people who were his main characters, and a description of Dachau today.

Wander, Fred   **The Seventh Well**
International Publishers, 1976 (paper)
This collection of short stories is set in Buchenwald concentration camp and is written by a Viennese survivor. Most of the stories are profiles of men that the author met in the camp; a 3-page story called "Bread" paints a verbal picture of the importance of bread to the prisoners so vivid that the reader can almost see and taste it. This piece would be a fine companion to Charlotte Delbo's passage on thirst.

47

Resistance

Bierman, John   **Righteous Gentile: The Story of Raoul Wallenberg, Missing Hero of the Holocaust**
> Viking, 1981
>
> The first part of Bierman's book chronicles Wallenberg's life—brief background on his youth, more detailed information on his activities in Budapest from July, 1944 to his disappearance in January of 1945. The estimates of the Jews he saved in these few months range from 30,000 to 100,000. Part II, which makes up almost half the book, discusses his disappearance and the attempt to locate him, including reports from people with information about him from shortly after his disappearance until the 1970s. Bierman stresses the failure of the Swedish, United States, Hungarian, and Israeli governments to adequately pursue the search. The author, a BBC-TV news correspondent, discovered the story while on assignment in Israel in 1979; he believes it possible that Wallenberg is still alive. [There are several other books about Wallenberg that are also recommended; brief bibliographic entries appear below.]

Dumbach, Annette E. & Newborn, Jud   **Shattering the German Night: The Story of the White Rose**
> Little, 1986
>
> The authors have recreated the history of the White Rose student resistance movement from letters, diaries, court records, and interviews with surviving relatives. Their account begins in 1942 and continues through the final execution,

There are several other books about Wallenberg that are also recommended:

Marton, Kati   **Wallenberg**
> Random, 1982
>
> The author is the daughter of Hungarian journalists who were arrested by the Russians, a former ABC correspondent, wife of Peter Jennings. Her account is perhaps the most personal and readable; she believes Wallenberg was alive in the mid-70s.

Rosenfeld, Harvey   **Raoul Wallenberg, Angel of Rescue**
> Prometheus, 1982
>
> Rosenfeld is editor of **Martyrdom & Resistance**, the longest-running periodical devoted to the Holocaust. This is the most scholarly work; Rosenfeld believes Wallenberg may still be alive.

Werkell, Frederick and Clarke, Thurston   **Lost Hero**
> McGraw-Hill, 1982
>
> Emphasis on Raoul Wallenberg's life, rather than the search; more information on Eichmann than the other books on Wallenberg. The authors believe Wallenberg died in the mid- sixties; their information is based on a report that the 3 other books quote as saying that Wallenberg was alive, but ill and in a mental hospital.

that of Willi Graf in October, 1943. They present sensitive portraits of the School family and other members of the White Rose — Alex Schmorell, Willi Graf, Christoph Probst, and Professor Karl Huber. This account not only provides a very human view of an important historical event, but also places it in the context of contemporary German and European history.

Flender, Harold　**Rescue in Denmark**
　　　Manor Books, 1963 (paper)
　　　This incredible story of Denmark's rescue of her Jewish citizens reads like a fairy tale, but it is actually well- documented fact; 98.5% of the Danish Jews were still alive after the war! The heroes of this resistance movement were people like Jorgen Knudsen, a young ambulance driver who went through the telephone directory checking off Jewish names and then "drove through Copenhagen calling on total strangers to give them the warning." The Jews were taken to Sweden by boat, and returned two years later to find their businesses running, their homes cleaned and painted, their pets and plants cared for. As the author says, "If there were a simple answer to the question - 'Why the Danes?' - we should be able to establish a formula for humanity."

Friedman, Philip　**Their Brothers' Keepers**
　　　Holocaust Library (Schocken), 1978 (paper)
　　　This is a welcome reissue of a book originally published in 1957, a history of the Christian men and women all over Europe who risked their lives to help rescue Jews. Friedman gives the political background of each country and discusses underground movements and rescue operations. Although some individuals are singled out, this is basically an overview rather than a collection of biographical essays.

Gies, Miep (with Alison Leslie Gols)　**Anne Frank Remembered**
　　　Simon & Schuster, 1987
　　　Miep was one of the people who helped to hide the Frank family. Her story fills in the gaps left by Anne's diary, not only by providing information on events outside the time frame of the diary, but, more significantly, on events outside the world of the Annex, thus putting the diary into historical perspective. Miep also tells her own story, and describes her husband's resistance activities, but emphasizes in her introduction that she does not consider herself a hero — 'my story is a story of very ordinary people during extraordinarily terrible times.'

Adult Books

Hallie, Philip   **Lest Innocent Blood Be Shed: The Story of the Village of Le Chambon and How Goodness Happened There**
Harper & Row, 1979
Le Chambon was a Protestant village in southern France; during the war, the village united under the leadership of Pastor André Trocmé to rescue thousands of Jewish children. The author of this book is a philosophy professor, and this is reflected in his work. In addition to telling the story of Pastor Trocmé and the village of Le Chambon, Professor Hallie writes extensively about the ethics of what happened there—about goodness and evil, theory and actions. It is less the story of what happened there than the philosophy of why it happened and a philosophical study of the man who inspired it.

Hanser, Richard   **A Noble Treason: The Revolt of the Munich Students Against Hitler**
Putnam, 1979
Hanser has written a detailed and readable account of the White Rose movement in Munich, one of the few examples of organized resistance to the Third Reich. Like any account of this movement, it is primarily the story of Hans and Sophie Scholl, the young brother and sister who led the movement and who were executed for treason. Other accounts are also listed in this bibliography, but this is the most in-depth look at the Scholls and the movement they represented. For other accounts, see Scholl's **Students Against Tyranny**, Dumbach and Newborn's **Shattering the German Night** and, in the children's section, Forman's **Ceremonies of Innocence**.

Hellman, Peter   **Avenue of the Righteous**
Atheneum, 1980
Four stories are included here, all accounts of "righteous gentiles" who helped rescue Jews—a Belgian woman, a Dutch family, a French store owner, and a Polish factory worker. The writing is flawed, but the characters in the stories are fascinating, especially Leokadia Jarmirska, the Polish woman who adopted and hid a Jewish baby while her husband spent the war years in Auschwitz.

Keneally, Thomas   **Schindler's List**
Simon & Schuster, 1982   (paper)
Oskar Schindler was a German industrialist with connections to high-ranking German officials and members of the SS. He used his influential position to save thousands of Jews, giving them work in his factory and protecting them from the Nazis. The information in the book is taken from interviews with many of those whom he saved, and presents a portrait of a complicated and compassionate human being who fought the system from within.

50

Ramati, Alexander   **The Assisi Underground: The Priest Who Rescued Jews**
Stein & Day, 1978
This is the story of an Italian priest who helped shelter Jews by providing them with fake identity cards and, after escape routes had closed, hiding Jews in the monasteries. He was a key part of the active Assisi underground, and enlisted the help of other clergy, townspeople, and once, an unwitting German officer. None of the Jews were captured, and the town was saved from destruction by a forged letter declaring it an open city. The author was one of the first journalists to enter Assisi after the Germans were driven out.

Scholl, Inge   **Students Against Tyranny**
Wesleyan University Press, 1970
This account of the lives of Hans and Sophie Scholl and the White Rose resistance movement was written by the Scholls' sister. Originally written for young people in 1952, this edition adds the texts of the leaflets published by the White Rose, and a number of documents, including the indictments and sentences of the Scholls and the others who were put on trial. In addition, it contains the text of a radio message broadcast at the time by Thomas Mann.

Senesh, Hannah   **Hannah Senesh: Her Life and Diary**
Schocken, 1971
Hannah Senesh was a Hungarian Jew who emigrated to Palestine in 1939; in 1944, she joined a rescue mission that parachuted into Hungary, where most of Hannah's family still lived. In the course of that mission, she was captured and later executed. Her diary covers the years from 1934 to January of 1944; it is followed by letters written to her family, the last ones shortly before she left on her mission. Following this are accounts from her contemporaries describing the mission and her capture, an essay written by her mother, and some of Hannah's poetry. Another version of her story, with much historical background on both Hungary and Palestine, is **The Summer That Bled** by Anthony Masters (St. Martin's, 1973).

Suhl, Yuri   **They Fought Back: The Story of the Jewish Resistance in Nazi Europe**
Schocken, 1975
Yuri Suhl has written several of the selections in this anthology himself, and some were written by historians specializing in this area. The rest are accounts by eyewitnesses and survivors, including at least one selection taken from the notes of a resistance fighter executed by the Nazis. In his introduction, Suhl states his purpose in collecting this material: "The full dramatic story of Jewish resistance to Nazism during World War II has yet to be told, and the need for telling it is now

more compelling than ever, not only to set the record down but also to set it straight." Most of the selections are brief and could be read by students.

Tec, Nchama   **When Light Pierced The Darkness: Christians Rescuing Jews in Nazi-occupied Poland**
Oxford, 1986
With information taken from published accounts, archival records, and personal interviews, Tec studies the Poles who rescued Jews — what motivated them, were they predominantly from one class, what common factors can be found? She explores the world of rescued and rescuer, and draws some significant conclusions, well summarized in her final chapter. Her introduction is an excellent overview of rescue activities in general, comparing and contrasting resistance in Denmark, Holland, and Belgium. Lengthy notes and bibliography.

Zassenhaus, Hiltgunt   **Walls: Resisting the Third Reich - One Woman's Story**
Beacon, 1974
While attending medical school, this German author also worked for the Nazi government, first as mail censor and then interpreter for Scandinavian POWs. Always opposed to Nazism, she used her first position to smuggle letters from prisoners to members of the resistance; her second position provided opportunities to take food, medicine, and hope to the prisoners. She is now a physician in the United States.

Art, Literature, and Literary Criticism

Alexander, Edward   **The Resonance of Dust: Essays on Holocaust Literature and Jewish Fate**
Ohio State U. Press, 1979
The book begins with a brief discussion of pre- Holocaust Jewish literature to illustrate the Jewish people's "unwillingness to credit . . . the existence of evil." Chapters are included on Isaac Bashevis Singer and Saul Bellow, on Israeli Holocaust fiction, and on American Jewish fiction. The author cites Donat's **Holocaust Kingdom** as "one of the most sustained attempts to analyze and evaluate the Jews' unpreparedness for believing in the reality of the horror directed against them." The emphasis is on views of Jewish religion and/or historical destiny.

Berenbaum, Michael   **The Vision of the Void: Theological Reflections on the Works of Elie Wiesel**
Wesleyan U. Press, 1979
The author was Jewish Chaplain at Wesleyan University and Deputy Director of the President's Commission on the Holocaust. He states that his intent in this book is "to pursue a systematic treatment of Wiesel's religious thought." He includes all of Weisel's works published to date, but, except for a chapter on **The Gates of the Forest**, arranges his material by theme rather than title. The book includes footnotes, index, and bibliography.

Blatter, Janet and Milton, Sybil   **Art of the Holocaust**
Rutledge Press, 1981
More than 350 works of art are reproduced in this volume; all were the creations of artists in ghettos, in hiding from the Nazis, or in the camps. The authors' commentary on each of the 150 artists help to place their work in historical perspecitve; in addition, they have included essays on Holocaust art, a preface by Irving Howe, and an historical overview by Henry Friedlander.

Ezrahi, Sidra Dekoven   **By Words Alone: The Holocaust in Literature**
U. of Chicago Press, 1980
Ms. Ezrahi is a lecturer at the Hebrew University of Jerusalem, and in this literary history she discusses the language of the Holocaust, documentation as art, what she refers to as "concentrationary realism," and the literature of survival. In

Adult Books

the latter half of the book, she deals with the Holocaust as Jewish tragedy, the Holocaust mythologized, and the Holocaust in American literature. The book includes notes, index, and bibliography.

Friedlander, Albert H. **Out of the Whirlwind: A Reader of Holocaust Literature**
    Doubleday, 1968
    This collection of excerpts includes a number of well- known Holocaust writers, among them Donat, Levi, and Wiesel—the prologue is by Wiesel. The book is divided thematically, and excerpts from one title may appear in more than one section. The final section is a series of articles by scholars and theologians on questions raised after and because of the Holocaust.

Fuchs, Elinor, ed.   **Plays of the Holocaust: an International Anthology**
    Theatre Communications Group, 1987
    Although numerous dramatic works on the Holocaust exist, this is the first major anthology of Holocaust drama. Each selection represents a different country, as well as different themes and styles, from black humor to realism and even fantasy. Selections are **Eli,** by Nelly Sachs; **Mister Fuge or Earth Sick**, by Liliane Atlan; **Auschwitz**, by Peter Barnes; **Ghetto**, by Joshua Sobol; **Replika**, by Josef Szajna, and **Cathedral of Ice**, by James Schevill. The book also includes an international bibliography of Holocaust drama by Alvin Goldfarb. Both the anthology and the bibliography are significant additions to Holocaust literature.

Green, Gerald   **The Artists of Terezin**
    Hawthorn, 1969, 1978
    The author of the television production **Holocaust** had originally written this volume in 1969; it was re-issued after the television and book versions of **Holocaust** achieved acclaim and aroused controversy. It is an account of the artists in Terezin concentration camp and their experiences, with numerous reproductions of their works; it includes material from **I Never Saw Another Butterfly**. The text is a readable and enlightening account of the camp, its inmates, and their art works.

Heinemann, Marlene   **Gender and Destiny: Women Writers and the Holocaust**
    Greenwood Press, 1986
    By the critical analysis of six works on the Holocaust by women writers, including Charlotte Delbo's **None of Us Will Return**, the author addresses the difference in male and female versions of the Holocaust. She focuses mainly on themes, characterization, peer relations, and authenticating strategies, while also pointing out the Nazi forms of assault on women.

YD3031

YD3031-7.8M-06-08-2021-7.48-G

UsedGood

Holocaust and Human Behavior:
Annotated Bibliography
(Discovering History and
Ourselves)

Heyen, William   **Erika: Poems of the Holocaust**
Vanguard, 1977 & 1984
Heyen's father emigrated from Germany in 1928, but his two brothers remained, both to fight and die in World War II, in the service of Germany. Heyen's poems reflect the torment this caused his father, and the emotion he himself felt about his uncles and his father's homeland. They also reflect the general horror of the Holocaust. The main value of these poems (and three prose pieces) is in the author's unique perspective. Some of the poems are moving and insightful, and would be appropriate for mature students. This volume includes those poems published earlier under the title **Swastika Poems.**

Hinz, Berthold   **Art in the Third Reich**
Pantheon, 1979
The author has written this history and analysis of National Socialist art in an effort to provide understanding of "the vast martialing of art and other aesthetic means in the Third Reich not as accidental elements, not as mere attractions or eccentricities, but as necessary conditions for the existence and political practice of a system suffering from an overwhelming lack of legitimization." The text discusses the history and analyzes the structure of art in Germany from 1933 to 1945, and is accompanied by numerous visual examples of the art and architecture of the period.

Insdorf, Annette   **Indelible Shadows: Film and the Holocaust**
Vintage Books, 1983
Seventy-five films are examined, including short films like **Night and Fog**, and feature films both American and foreign. Dr. Insdorf discusses whether these films express or evade the issues of the Holocaust, the development of a suitable language, and a variety of narrative strategies. Included are chapters on "The Hollywood Version of the Holocaust" and "The New German Guilt." It is an illuminating and insightful work that reflects the author's expertise in both film and Holocaust studies.

Kamenetsky, Christa   **Children's Literature in Hitler's Germany: The Cultural Policy of National Socialism**
Ohio University Press, 1984
The author traces the Nazi attempt to control children's reading from the roots of children's folk literature in pre-Nazi Germany to Nazi attempts to control libraries and publishers. She covers not only censorship itself, but the way material was selected and adapted from existing literature—folktales, myths, sagas, classics, etc. Material that supported the Nazi philosophy was carefully worked into children's primers and readers. The new literature, the glorification of the peasant warrior, school reform, library control, and many other issues are discussed in

depth. This history is fascinating, but terrifying— except for the fact that the Third Reich did not last long enough to test the effectiveness of this approach, this could be a how-to handbook in mind control. The author handles her subject in a thorough and scholarly manner, with many notes, a bibliography and index.

Langer, Lawrence L.   **The Age of Atrocity: Death in Modern Literature**
Beacon, 1978
In the words of the author, "This book is concerned with the evolution of the idea of atrocity in the twentieth century, and the attempt of a few significant writers to assess its influence on our conception of the human image." It is a monumental subject, and a monumental book, essential reading for anyone who seeks to understand how the Holocaust and other modern atrocities have altered our conceptions of life and death and humanity. The writers selected are Thomas Mann, Albert Camus, Alexander Solzhenitsyn, and Charlotte Delbo; the discussion moves progressively from the death of an individual, as portrayed in Mann's **Magic Mountain**, to the deaths of multitudes, death by atrocity, and death by extermination.

Langer, Lawrence L.   **The Holocaust and the Literary Imagination**
Yale, 1975
This is a scholarly work of literary criticism, organized around "recurrent themes that illustrate the aesthetic problems of reconciling normalcy with horror." The author selects a few titles from the "literature of atrocity," among them Elie Wiesel's **Night** and André Schwarz- Bart's **The Last of the Just**; although the former book is autobiographical rather than fictional, Langer defines it as literature, due to its "compressed imaginative power and artful presentation." In analyzing these works and others, he draws parallels to other literary works, particularly those of Kafka and Camus. He describes this type of literature as "art for history's sake which is not historical art or fiction, but conceals the features of history behind an imaginative mask . . ."

Rhodes, Anthony   **Propaganda - The Art of Persuasion: World War II**
Chelsea, 1976
Joseph Goebbels said, "Nothing is easier than leading the people on a leash. I just hold up a campaign poster and they jump through it." This book is a catalog of posters from Germany, Italy, Great Britain, the United States, Russia, and Japan. The text discusses political propaganda and its uses in films, art, literature, music, and the theater, in addition to posters. The text is minimal, however, in comparison with the many reproductions of posters, leaflets, stamps, and magazine covers. Students and teachers alike will find that this volume adds a further dimension to the understanding of the uses and effects of propaganda, simply in the visual impact of the posters themselves.

Rosenfeld, Alvin H. & Greenberg, Irving, eds.   **Confronting the Holocaust: The Impact of Elie Wiesel**
Indiana University Press, 1978
This collection of critical essays includes contributions by Lawrence L. Langer, Terrence Des Pres, and a number of others. It is a scholarly work on a variety of themes dealing with the Holocaust, Jewish tradition, Holocaust literature in general, and Wiesel's work in particular. It concludes with a wonderful essay by Wiesel himself, entitled "Why I Write."

Rosenfeld, Alvin H.   **A Double Dying: Reflections on Holocaust Literature**
Indiana University Press, 1980
The title is derived from an Elie Wiesel quote: "At Auschwitz, not only man died, but also the idea of man." Rosenfeld discusses many books, from **Night** to **Sophie's Choice**, diaries as well as novels. He includes more authors in less detail than most works of literary criticism, and new authors, like Leslie Epstein and Sylvia Plath, who, along with Styron, come in the final chapter, called "Exploiting Atrocity."

Sachs, Nelly   **O the Chimneys**
Farrar, Straus & Giroux, 1967
Nelly Sachs was a German Jew who fled to Sweden in 1940. She said that all she had left was language, and she used her last possession to create, in poetry, a testimonial to her people. The poems are filled with grief, pain, and death, but they also reflect love, hope, and a deep, abiding faith. The author's strong background in Jewish literary and religious tradition is evident throughout, especially in "Eli," a mystery play included in this volume. The poems are printed in both German and English; a second volume of her poetry, **The Seeker**, was published in 1970.

Szonyi, David M., ed.   **Holocaust: An Annotated Bibliography and Resource Guide**
Ktav, 1985
A comprehensive bibliography, this begins with Jewish life before the Holocaust, includes sections on German responses, Jewish resistance, the response of the churches, and many other subjects, as well as special sections on literature, young people's literature, and audio-visual materials and music resources. It is especially useful to anyone needing more sources on a particular subject. In addition to the bibliographies, there are sections on exhibits, institutes, memorials, education programs, survivor groups, remembrance services, oral history, speakers, and fundings. This is an invaluable guide for the serious student of the Holocaust.

Nazi Education

Mann, Erika   **School for Barbarians**
            Modern Age, 1938
            Erika Mann was the daughter of Thomas Mann; the entire Mann family
left Germany shortly after Hitler's rise to power. In his introduction to his
daughter's book, Thomas Mann says that the reader will see "a comprehensive and
fully informed portrayal of the totalitarian state" through this study of education in
Germany. The book is not an objective documentation of the facts, although the
facts are there; it is a personal statement about the effects of those fundamental
changes on the people and the culture of the country she loves, and her faith that
the people will one day regain the "sense of justice and humanity [that] is being
stolen from them."

Ziemer, Gregor   **Education for Death: The Making of a Nazi**
            Octagon, 1972
            The author of this volume was president of an American school in Ger-
many before the war; as such, he received permission from the German authorities
to visit their schools. When he returned to the United States he wrote this book
describing in detail the Nazi educational system, from preschool to the university.
Originally published in 1941, the book concludes with a plea to American educators to demonstrate that "education for life is more worthy of survival than Hitler's
education for death."

Hitler and Nazism

This section of the bibliography has been included as a result of numerous requests for information about the Nazis, and specifically about Hitler. It was added with great reluctance, and with the warning that these books should be used with as much caution as the "glorious adventure" stories for children. Hitler and Nazism have a fascination that can distract the reader from the real issues of the Holocaust, and can even be a way of avoiding those issues. At least one historian has stated that the fascination with Hitler may be a way of avoiding the horrors of the Holocaust, of shifting the focus from things too painful to pursue. If a serious study of the behavior of Hitler and the Nazis can help the reader better understand humanity and inhumanity, can aid in the effort to face both history and one's self, then these books serve a purpose. Otherwise, such a study is, at best, an intellectual exercise; at worst, a distortion of the truths that history can teach us, a concentrated view from the wrong end of the telescope.

Bullock, Alan   **Hitler: A Study in Tyranny**
Harper & Row, 1964
Bullock's book is probably the best for the reader who wants to put the Holocaust into historical context in terms of German history. The author shows clearly the relationship between Hitler and the Nazi Party, and traces the roots of Nazism and many of its policies back to the Weimar Republic. Those readers who feel that they need some historical background information on Hitler and Nazism in order to understand the Holocaust, but who do not want to concentrate in this area, will find that Bullock's book should provide all the information that they need.

Cocks, Geoffrey **Psychotherapy in the Third Reich: The Goering Institute**
Oxford University Press, 1985
The Goering Institute was run by Matthias Heinrich Goering, the cousin of the Reichsmarshall; this work relates the history of the institute and its contribution to the development of psychotherapy in Central Europe during the Third Reich. It is the author's opinion that psychotherapy achieved its highest professional status during this period. This is an excellent companion to Robert J. Lifton's **Nazi Doctors.**

Adult Books

Fest, Joachim C **Hitler**
Harcourt Brace, 1973
No one but the serious student will want to read more than 750 pages on Hitler, but Fest's book is both readable and well-indexed for easy references. George Mosse has called it "monumental" and "the most balanced of such books, even though it too focuses on the leader to the neglect of other historical forces." Fest is a German journalist who fought in the German armed forces in World War II.

Fleming, Gerald **Hitler and the Final Solution**
University of California Press, 1982
This well-researched history is a response to Irving's revisionist theory that Hitler knew nothing about the "Final Solution," at least until 1943 or 1944. Based on material from British, American, and Soviet archives, Fleming makes a strong case for the idea that Hitler not only knew about, but was instrumental in planning and implementing, the "Final Solution."

Goebbels, Joseph **Final Entries 1945: The Diaries of Joseph Goebbels**
Putnam, 1978
Earlier diaries of Goebbels, some going back to 1926, have been published; the last chapters, however, represented in this volume, present a dramatic picture of the end of the Reich. To the end, Goebbels maintained faith in the Führer; as stated in a New York Times review, "Goebbels's mind remained locked in a mirror-chamber of his own Nazi propaganda." The diary ends on April 9, 1945; Goebbels committed suicide on May 1, following the suicide of Hitler.

Haffner, Sebastian **The Meaning of Hitler: Hitler's Uses of Power, His Successes and Failures**
Macmillan, 1979
Haffner is a German historian and journalist; the book deals not with historical facts, but, as the title indicates, with their meaning. His ideas are controversial, as are most recent books on Hitler. Alan Bullock describes this, in the New York Review of Books, as "bold in its ideas ... never dropping the level of intellectual tension." Although Bullock disagrees with many of Haffner's theories, he calls the book engrossing and credits Haffner for his "gift of expressing ideas ... with directness and vigor ..."

Heston, Leonard L. and Heston, Renate   **The Medical Casebook of Adolf Hitler**
Introduction by Albert Speer
Stein & Day, 1979
Leonard Heston is a psychiatry professor, his wife a German-born psychiatric nurse. After much research they have provided a thoroughly documented study of Hitler's medical history, along with an unproven theory that the last three or four years of his life, he was dependent on amphetamines. Speer accepts this as a plausible explanation, but states that, in his opinion, it did not change either Hitler's aims or the course of history. "Power itself was the main drug underlying his activity ..."

Hoess, Rudolf   **Commandant of Auschwitz**
World, 1959
Hoess wrote this autobiography in prison in 1947; it covers his life from childhood to his arrest. He provides revealing, and at times incredible, accounts of his term as block leader at Dachau and as commandant of Auschwitz. He talks, for example, about the Gypsies being his "best-loved prisoners," whom he would have studied more closely if they had not been scheduled for extermination, and he admits to feeling "uncomfortable" the first time he witnessed the gassing of prisoners. He concludes with his opinion of the Third Reich and the exterminations, and his own role.

Irving, David   **Hitler's War**
Viking, 1977
Irving describes Hitler as "an ordinary walking, talking, human ..."; he shows greater indignation at the bombing of Hamburg than at the extermination of the Jews. His main theme in this 900-page work, however, is that Hitler did not order the exterminations and was not even aware of them until 1943 or 1944; he places the responsibility for these acts on Himmler. The closest he will come to involving Hitler at all is to state that he may have possessed a conscious desire "not to know."

Koonz, Claudia   **Mothers in the Fatherland: Women, the Family, and Nazi Politics**
St. Martins, 1987
The role of women in Nazi Germany, Hitler's attitude toward women, and the distinction between male and female roles are the focal points for this detailed, in-depth study. The history of the women's movement and its leaders, from the Weimar years to the begininings of the Nazi era is well-researched and supported by lengthy notes and an extensive bibliography. Koonz goes beyond this, though, to describe the roles of both Protestant and Catholic women, and the women's movements within those institutions. She also includes two chapters that are less

well-documented, due to the lack of records, on women resisters and on Jewish women. Throughout the book, she deals with the effect of Nazism on the family unit, as well as on women specifically. Although this is a lengthy and scholarly work, it is also a personal and readable one, an important contribution to both Holocaust and Feminist studies.

Lifton, Robert J.   **Nazi Doctors: Medical Killing and the Psychology of Genocide**
Basic Books, 1986
A comprehensive study of Nazi doctors, both in the concentration camps and the "euthanasia" program, this is based on interviews with Nazi doctors, prisoner doctors, and survivors, as well as archival records of the concentration camps and Nazi medical institutions. In the concluding section Lifton offers a psychological explanation of how the doctors, trained to save lives, could cope with participation in the daily evil of the camps. In addition to providing insights into the medical profession during the Third Reich, Lifton raises significant questions about medical ethics in the postwar decades.

Mandell, Richard D.   **The Nazi Olympics**
Macmillan, 1971
Mandell, now an Associate Professor of History at the University of South Carolina, was formerly a factory worker and technical writer in Germany. He states his belief in the preface that " ... much of the success of the 1936 Olympics was due to the pursuit by the National Socialists of supremacy in mass pageantry. Hitler's success as a whole is inconceivable without the application of the contrived festivity that enveloped the Nazis from beginning to end." He gives the history and politics of the Olympics, as well as a full account of the games. His plea is to remove some of the patriotic rites from the Olympics, so that they can never again be used as a political technique.

Merkl, Peter   **The Making of a Storm Trooper**
Princeton U. Press, 1980
Although the author concludes that the motivation of the stormtroopers (SA) were too complex and individual to be reduced to one simple factor, his study does help explain the historical, social, political, and psychological motives that led young men into the SA, and the circumstances under which this organization became so powerful. This is enlightening, not only with regard to the stormtroopers themselves; it may have bearing on the rise of other violent socio-political move-ments.

Reitlinger, Gerald   **The SS: Alibi of a Nation, 1922-1945**
Viking, 1957
Beginning with a brief overview of the SS and the SA in their early stages, the author concentrates on the origins, development, and functions of the SS. He discusses the organization both as a political police force and as concentration camp guards; there are also several chapters on Himmler and his involvement with the SS. The title derives from a belief of the author that the Nuremberg Tribunal, by declaring the SS a criminal organization, provided the German nation with a "convenient scapegoat"; in truth, there was no way that the SS could have operated without the support of the entire German bureaucracy.

Sereny, Gita   **Into That Darkness: From Mercy Killing to Mass Murder**
McGraw-Hill, 1974
Ms. Sereny has told the story of Franz Stangl from interviews she held with him while he was in prison in 1971, as a Nazi war criminal. His story is told in six parts: Hartheim, a euthanasia center and Stangl's first important assignment; Sobibor, an extermination camp; Treblinka, where he was Kommandant; the end of the war; his escape from Germany; his life in Brazil until his arrest in 1967. In each section she includes testimony of other witnesses. This is probably the best and the most enlightening portrait of a Nazi.

Speer, Albert   **Inside the Third Reich**
Macmillan, 1970 (paper, Avon)
Albert Speer was a Nazi Minister, the only Nazi to admit guilt at the Nuremberg trials. He joined the Nazi party in 1939, and his book traces the rise of Hitler and the Party as well as his own involvement. Speer wrote most of this book in prison, where he served a 20-year sentence as a result of his conviction at Nuremberg. He waived the right to appeal and served his full term; he was released in 1966, but in his own words, the account of atrocity that he heard at the trial "has outlasted the verdict of the court." He died in 1981 in Great Britain.

Stone, Norman   **Hitler**
Little Brown, 1980
More history than biography, by a historian young enough to view the war with the detachment with which many historians look at World War I. It is shorter than Irving's book, and more easily read; it offers no new historical evidence, but puts an emphasis on Hitler's positive achievements and the Russian contribution to the war's end. As revisionist history, it is more objective and faithful to tradition than most.

Adult Books

Toland, John   **Adolf Hitler**
Doubleday, 1976 (paper, Ballantine)
In more than 1,000 pages the author describes the life of Hitler, presenting his "admirable" qualities as well as the evil. The book is well-researched, but Toland seems to accept his sources at face value, with little questioning or serious analysis. The Saturday Review states, "Bullock and Fest deal with materials in a critical, questioning spirit that challenges thought. Toland simply tells a dramatic story."

von Lang, Joseph   **The Secretary: Martin Bormann, the Man Who Manipulated Hitler**
Random House, 1979
As well as tracking down the rumors about Bormann's death, the author details his life, with an accumulation of trivia that the New York Times reviewer says "underscores, by extension," Hannah Arendt's well-known phrase "the banality of evil." Von Lang, a German writer, leaves no doubt that the extermination orders, to Bormann and others, were issued by Hitler, David Irving's claim notwithstanding.

Judgment

Arendt, Hannah   **Eichmann in Jerusalem: A Report on the Banality of Evil**
Viking, 1963 (revised ed., 1965)
Ms. Arendt was the center of much controversy when this book was first published, chiefly due to her claim that Eichmann was not the epitome of evil that many would like to believe, but merely a common petty bureaucrat. She also raised controversy by her criticism of Jewish leaders in Europe during the war. She reviews Eichmann's involvement with the deportations and exterminations, and in a postscript discusses the uproar aroused by her ideas even before the publication of the book. She also expands upon her often-quoted phrase, "the banality of evil."

Conot, Robert   **Justice at Nuremberg**
Harper & Row, 1984
The proceedings at Nuremberg, and the history revealed through them, are covered in depth here, but Conot goes beyond this to examine in detail the preparations for the Tribunal and the complications of an international legal body. He points out the way personalities, as well as differences in legal and political systems, necessitated compromise and impinged on judgment.

Ferencz, Benjamin   **Less Than Slaves: Jewish Forced Labor and the Quest for Compensation**
Harvard University Press, 1979
The issue addressed here is that of reparations for the slave labor provided by Jewish survivors for major industrialists like I.G. Farben. The fundamental questions raised are why executives of these firms were given such light sentences, why the managers were not held accountable, and why restitution to the victims has been either inadequate or nonexistent.

Hausner, Gideon   **Justice in Jerusalem**
Harper, 1966 (paper, Holocaust Library/Schocken)
Hausner was Attorney General of Israel when Eichmann was charged and brought to trial. As such, he became prosecutor at the trial. He provides a personal, detailed account of the trial and of Eichmann himself, as well as supplying historical background material. The appendix includes reactions to the trial.

Adult Books

Neave, Airey **On Trial at Nuremberg**
Little Brown, 1978
Neave was a member of the British War Crimes Executive Team in 1945.
He was a lawyer, had lived and studied in Germany, served in the RAF, and
escaped from a German POW camp. He was selected to serve the indictments to
those who were tried at Nuremberg. The bulk of the book is not a description of the
trial itself, but of the serving of the indictments, and the author's personal impres-
sions of each of the defendants. He then discusses the judges, the prosecuting
attorney, the verdicts, and his own views on the legitimacy and value of the trial
itself.

Ryan, Allan A., Jr. **Quiet Neighbors: Prosecuting Nazi War Criminals in
America**
Harcourt Brace Jovanovich, 1984
Ryan is a former director of the U.S. Office of Special Investigation; his
interest in Nazi war criminals focused on those who had come to the U.S. and
settled in comfortably as "quiet neighbors." He traces the deeds of such men as
Klaus Barbie and Ivan Demjanjuk, and describes the difficulties of bringing such
men to justice.

Saidel, Rochelle G. **Outraged Conscience: Seekers of Justice for Nazi War
Criminals in America**
SUNY Press, 1984
In this study of those who have dedicated their lives to seeking out Nazi
war criminals in the U.S., Saidel includes not only well-known figures like Simon
Wiesenthal, but lesser-known individuals who have given up their careers to devote
their full attention to this work. It is a fascinating, readable account that raises
disturbing questions about the reactions of Americans to these efforts.

Schwarberg, Gunther **Murders at Bullenhuser Damm**
Indiana University Press, 1984
On April 20, 1945, twenty Jewish children were hanged by the SS. The
doctor in charge, who ordered the execution to cover up medical experimentation,
was tried and sentenced to life imprisonment. The SS Kommandant implicated in
this crime, however, Arnold Strippel, remains free in West Germany. In this
monograph, Schwarberg describes the unsuccessful efforts of the children's
relatives to bring Strippel to justice, and also discusses the difficulty Germans have
in coming to terms with the Holocaust.

Simpson, Christopher   **Blowback: The U.S. Recruitment of Nazis—and the Long-Range Effect on the Cold War**
    Weidenfeld and Nicolson, New York, 1988
    Blowback offers a full description of how the U.S. government recruited Nazis and war criminals to serve American intelligence agencies after WWII. Using recently released documents, Simpson discloses how top ranking American officials participated in the effort to bring Nazis and collaborators into the U.S. He not only shows how the U.S. made use of Nazis in European operations such as Paperclip and Operation Gehlen, but he also brings to light how the U.S. government sanctioned the immigration of thousands of former Nazis into the U.S., who in turn, had influence on the course of American domestic and foreign policy.

Smith, Bradley F.   **Reaching Judgment at Nuremberg**
    Basic Books, 1977
    After two chapters of background material, the author devotes three chapters to trial and judgment, and over a third of the book to individual verdicts. In addition to the actual proceedings and decisions, he discusses the background of the judges, the attitudes and considerations that led to the decisions. Twenty-six pages of notes for a 300-page book testify to the careful documentation of this work.

Uris, Leon   **QB VII**
    Doubleday, 1970 (paper, Bantam)
    This intriguing, suspenseful novel concerns a well- known writer whose book about the Holocaust names an eminent doctor as having been involved in medical atrocities at a concentration camp. This sets the scene for a dramatic trial, as the doctor seeks to exonerate himself. Uris is a master storyteller, and through the vehicle of the novel form, he raises the issues of judgment and justice.

German Culture

No study of the Holocaust, or of any other example of man's inhumanity, could be called comprehensive if it focused its attention solely on the victim. Neither is it enough to study the leaders, whether they are dismissed as maniacs or analyzed in terms of strategy, propaganda campaigns and military techniques. In order to understand what happened in Germany in the 1930s, it is necessary to take a careful look at the culture then and in the preceding decade, less from the aspect of scholarly historical research than from looking at the real lives of real people. As Otto Friedrich states in the work listed below, "The desire to live one's life as best one can, to do one's work and raise one's own children, is not a contemptible emotion." And to understand the ordinary Berliner in 1933, one can only try to imagine what one might do himself in a similar situation.

The study of German culture is twofold; the dictionary defines "culture" in two ways—the intellectual and artistic expression of a society, and the social behavior characteristic of a people. The titles listed below explore both aspects of German culture, that of the ordinary citizen and that of the academic and artistic community. Some of them simply describe life in the twenties and thirties, some examine the dynamics between that life and the rise of Nazism, and a few go beyond to attempt to find causes, cures and conclusions. In the last area, William Sheridan Allen's final paragraph contains valuable words for all who seek to understand what happened in Germany: "Each group saw one or the other side of Nazism, but none saw it in its full hideousness ... The problem of Nazism was primarily a problem of perception. In this respect Thalburg's difficulties and Thalburg's fate are likely to be shared by other men in other towns under similar circumstances. The remedy will not be easily found."

Holocaust and Human Behavior Bibliography

Allen, William Sheridan   **The Nazi Seizure of Power: The Experience of a Single German Town, 1930-1945**
Quadrangle, 1965 (paper, New Viewpoints)
Thirty years after the events described in the book, Dr. Allen went to a small town in Germany in an attempt to reconstruct the climate that existed there in the years immediately preceding and following Hitler's rise to power. The name of the town (called Thalburg in the book) and the names of specific people were changed in this published version of Allen's doctoral dissertation. While he admits that the town was by no means average, his detailed documentation of the causes and effects of Nazism in one community is an illuminating microcosm in the study of totalitarianism.

de Jonge, Alex   **The Weimar Chronicle**
Paddington Press, 1978
The author's intent, as stated in his preface (where he also states his personal biases as reflected in the book), is to bring back to life the Germany of the twenties, as a chronicler rather than a historian. He quotes heavily from eyewitness accounts and newspaper clippings. After re-creating the mood of the times that led many to welcome Hitler, he deliberately and appropriately concludes with an eyewitness account of Hitler's torchlight procession into Berlin in 1933.

Engelman, Bernt   **In Hitler's Germany: Everyday Life in the Third Reich**
Pantheon, 1986
The author grew up in Nazi Germany, in a family opposed to Hitler and Nazism; here, he interweaves his own story with those of other Germans who lived through this era, both Nazis and non-Nazis. He describes those who truly believed and those who were almost totally unaware of what was happening. He also describes resistance activities, from the tailor who helped smuggle out refugees to his own activities in the Luftwaffe. Condensed from the two-volume German edition, with a foreword by Studs Terkel.

Ericksen, Robert P.   **Theologians Under Hitler: Gerhard Kittel, Paul Althaus, and Emmanuel Hirsch**
Yale University Press, 1985
The author presents the careers and intellectual biographies of three prominent German theologians who supported Hitler to different degrees and for different reasons. Although more narrowly focused than Heimreich's book, it provides good case studies of the accommodation of the educated middle class to Nazism.

69

Friedrich, Otto   **Before the Deluge: A Portrait of Berlin in the 1920s**
Harper & Row, 1972 (paper, Avon)
This portrait of Berlin is not, like the Allen book, a work of detailed historical research. It could almost be called nostalgia. Its pages teem with names still well known in artistic and intellectual circles: Rudolph Serkin, Albert Einstein, Arthur Koestler, the Bauhaus school of architecture, and many more—artists, musicians, playwrights, filmmakers, and film stars. Interwoven with accounts and anecdotes of this part of Berlin society in the twenties and early thirties is an account of the rise of Nazism and its effect on the nation in general and the artistic and intellectual community in particular.

Gay, Peter   **Weimar Culture: The Outsider as Insider**
Harper & Row, 1968
Peter Gay was a German Jew exiled by Hitler, who later became a member of the history department at Yale University; thus both by profession and background he is eminently qualified to write the story of Weimar culture. As in Friedrich's book, the focus is on artistic and intellectual Germany, but this is broader in scope and more scholarly in approach. There is also a stronger emphasis on the academic community, and on the parallel course of Weimar culture and Weimar politics.

Helmreich, Ernst Christian   **The German Church Under Hitler: Background, Struggle, and Epilogue**
Wayne State University Press, 1979
A prominent German religious historian describes the movements and conflicts within the German churches that often confused or delayed opposition to Nazism. He analyzes the Deutsche Christen, which came to terms with Nazism, and the Confessional Church, which opposed it. He also discusses those who took positions between these two extremes, and discusses the role of the Roman Catholic Church, as well as many smaller sects.

Henry, Frances   **Victims and Neighbors: A Small Town in Nazi Germany Remembered**
Begin & Garvey, 1984
Sonderburg is a small town in Southern Germany, and like Thalburg in Allen's **Nazi Seizure of Power**, the name of the town is fictitious. The town itself was real, however, and was the home of the author's grandparents, a place she visited as a child. She emigrated to the U.S. at age 7; her return to Sonderberg in 1975 inspired the research project that resulted in this book, a study of relations between Jew and Gentile before and after Nazism. She interviews Germans still living in Sonderburg and Jewish survivors now living in the U.S., describing the degree of integration (she distinguishes between integration and assimilation,

which she feels did not occur), as well as prejudice before 1933, and the efforts of the villagers toward the Jews afterwards. Her findings are probably typical of many German small towns, and the book is an excellent companion to Allen's, adding to his study of interpersonal relations within a similar structure.

Isherwood, Christopher   **The Berlin Stories**
New Directions, 1935, 1954
The author is an Englishman who spent four years in Berlin, from 1929 to 1933; he went there mainly to visit his old friend W.H. Auden. While in Berlin Isherwood kept a detailed diary which later became the raw material for these stories, originally published separately between 1935 and 1939. One of the stories, "Sally Bowles," was later adapted by John van Druten into the play **I Am a Camera**, which in turn became the musical Cabaret. The stories are generally considered fiction, but could more actually be called dramatized memoirs, and as such contribute greatly to the social history of the period. In the introduction to the 1954 edition, the author describes his return to Berlin in 1952 and compares that Berlin with the one he knew.

Lang, Daniel   **A Backward Look: Germans Remember**
McGraw-Hill, 1979
This book was at least partially inspired by a project the author learned of involving a teacher in Germany who brought his class of 15-year-olds together with men who had been their age during the Hitler years. The teacher wrote a book about this project and Lang got in touch with him; with the teacher's help, Lang went to Germany to talk with Germans about their memories of those years. This is shorter, more informal, and more readable than **They Thought They Were Free**, and would appeal to young people and others who want a brief "backward look."

Mann, Erika   **The Lights Go Down**
Farrar & Rinehart, 1940
Erika Mann was the daughter of Thomas Mann and the wife of W.H. Auden, as well as an author and actress in her own right. She was part of the society that Friedrich and Gay described and that Isherwood became a part of through his friendship with Auden. This work, which could most appropriately be called a documentary novel, was published in 1940, after the Mann family had fled Germany; the paperback version is subtitled **Middletown - Nazi Version**. The author paints a verbal portrait of a German town by telling of nine of its residents and one stranger passing through, stories of a middle-class German town and the effect Nazism had on the lives of its people. Each episode is written as a short story, but the factual documentation of relevant historical facts is provided at the end of the book. [See note on the Mann family at the end of this section.]

German Culture

Mayer, Milton   **They Thought They Were Free: The Germans, 1933-1945**
University of Chicago Press, 1955
An American newsman of German-Jewish descent, the author spent a year in Germany after the war, trying to find out "what the Nazi had been and how he got that way." In a German town he called Kronenberg, he met ten men, none "average" but all sufficiently different from one another to be representative—from baker to policeman to schoolteacher. He probes into the past with these men, seeking both historical fact and personal actions and reactions. In the latter part of the book he discusses the German people in general, based on the perspective of the preceding section, and concludes with several chapters on the postwar years.

Meinecke, Friedrich   **The German Catastrophe**
Beacon Press, 1963
The author, who died in 1954, was a noted German historian; this book was written shortly after the war, and is a scholarly look at its causes, in historical terms. As well as discussing Hitlerism, the author writes about aspects of German culture and politics that made Hitlerism possible, and whether it happened by chance or was inevitable.

Mosse, George L.   **Nazi Culture: Intellectual, Cultural and Social Life in the Third Reich**
Universal Library (Grosset & Dunlap), 1966
The first section, "Hitler Sets the Tone," is mainly the author's own work; the following sections are original source material, with an introduction by the author. Areas covered include militarism, family life, womanhood, racism, heroes and myths, intellectuals, science, religion, education, and others. Contributors include Martin Bormann, Joseph Goebbels, Adolf Hitler, and many lesser-known Germans. These documents help to demonstrate what it was like to live in Nazi Germany, whatever one's role in society.

Peukert, Detlev J.K.   **Inside Nazi Germany: Conformity, Opposition and Racism in Everyday Life**
Yale University Press, 1987
This is a translation of a work originally published in Germany in 1982. The author provides a social history of the Third Reich, in which he surveys the experiences and attitudes of ordinary Germans and the ways in which they responded to the demands of the Nazi regime

Porter, Katherine Anne   **The Leaning Tower and Other Stories**
Harcourt, 1944 (paper, NAL)
The title story in this collection is actually a novella rather than a short story, almost a hundred pages long. It is the story of a young American artist who visited Berlin in the winter of 1931-32. He had chosen Berlin because his closest childhood friend had been German and had painted vivid images of the glamour of that city. Charles' friend died, but the images remained and finally led him to Berlin; the images did not, however, seem to fit the Berlin that Charles found in 1931.

Shirer, William   **Nightmare Years 1930-1940. Vol. II**
Little Brown, 1984
Shirer spent much of his time as a young journalist in Berlin, where he witnessed Hitler's rise to power. Drawing on diaries that he kept during that time, he describes his observations, his feelings, and his attempts to warn others through his broadcasts.

The Ten Commandments: Ten Short Novels of Hitler's War Against the Moral Code
Simon & Schuster, 1943
The editor's foreword states, "It is my hope that this book - Thomas Mann's story of the man who gave the world the Ten Commandments, and the other nine stories dealing with the men who have sought to destroy those Commandments - will help to open the eyes of those who still do not recognize what Nazism really is." Among the authors, in addition to Mann, were Franz Werfel and Bruno Frank, who were also German exiles; the other authors are Rebecca West, Sigrid Undset, Andre Maurois, Louis Bromfield, Jules Romains, John Erskine, and Hendrik Willem van Loon. This is a unique piece of highly literary propaganda.

Tucholsky, Kurt   **Deutschland, Deutschland Über Alles**
University of Massachusetts Press, 1972
Tucholsky was a critic, novelist and satirist in Germany in the twenties and early thirties; he committed suicide in Sweden in 1935. This work was originally published in 1929; it is a collection of bitter satirical essays, poems and photographs on a variety of subjects, from the national economy and the Reichstag to fashion queens and the reason why mailboxes have to be ugly.

German Culture

Vassiltchikov, Marie   **Berlin Diaries, 1940-1945**
Knopf, 1987
The diaries of an exiled white Russian princess who worked for both the German Broadcasting Corporation and the German Foreign Office provide little information on the Holocaust, but numerous insights about wartime conditions in Berlin. The descriptions of the princess's social circle are probably the most interesting parts of the diaries; in that circle were both aristocrats and anti-Nazis, several of whom took part in, or fell victims to, the aftermath of the July 20, 1944 plot to kill Hitler.

Wilkinson, James D. **The Intellectual Resistance in Europe**
Harvard University Press, 1981
This is a survey of intellectual resistance in three countries—France, Germany, and Italy. Wilkinson discusses the role of writers in these countries during the war, concentrating mainly on Camus, Sartre and de Beauvoir in France and Dietrich Bonhoeffer in Germany. The Italian section is probably the most enlightening, being less well known, at least in the United States—Silone, Vittorini, and Pavese. Wilkinson also addresses himself to the issue of Resistance idealism after the war, and why the unity of the intellectuals gave way to the reestablishment of the conservative status quo.

Wolfe, Thomas **You Can't Go Home Again** Chapter 38, "The Dark Messiah"
Harper, 1940
In the latter part of Thomas Wolfe's epic autobiographical novel, the protagonist, George Webber, goes to Germany to celebrate the publication of the German edition of his book. It is 1936, and his last visit to Germany had been in 1929. With the eyes of an outsider and the pen of a consummate writer, these few pages capsulize the intrinsic nature of Nazi Germany.

Note: The family of Thomas Mann have provided a rich source of material for those interested in the German intellectual scene before and during the war. In addition to the two books by Erika Mann listed in this bibliography, and the collection of stories, **The Ten Commandments**, to which Thomas Mann himself was a contributor, Mann's son Klaus wrote a novel, **Mephisto** (1936, reissued in 1977), and an autobiography, **The Turning Point** (1942). Erika and Klaus Mann wrote two books together, **Escape to Life** (1939) and **The Other Germany** (1940); **Unwritten Memories**, by Mann's wife Katia, was published in 1975, compiled from taped interviews by her son Michael and Elisabeth Plessen. Mann himself published the text of a lecture given on a coast-to-coast tour of the United States, **The Coming Victory of Democracy** (1938). A study of the Mann family's works provides a fascinating portrait of a family and an era. For those who wonder what American novelists were thinking and writing about events in Germany, Erika and Klaus mention three books: **Winter in April** by Robert Nathan (1937), **The Mortal Storm** by Phyllis Bottome (1938), and **It Can't Happen Here** by Sinclair Lewis (1935); they also make note of the journalistic writings of Dorothy Thompson. Perhaps the most distinguished fictional treatment of the evil of Nazi Germany is Thomas Mann's own postwar novel, **Doctor Faustus**.

Genocide of the Armenian People

The Armenian Genocide presents a completely different problem in terms of literature, both juvenile and adult, from that of Holocaust literature. Although there are many books about World War II that gloss over or ignore the Holocaust, there are also a large number, both fiction and non-fiction, that qualify as Holocaust literature. The problem is not one of searching for material, but of selecting the best and most appropriate material for the needs and interests of the reader. Holocaust literature is so extensive that selectivity becomes a mandate, not an option; not even the most avid reader could cover more than a fraction of the books available.

Conversely, literature on the Armenian Genocide, especially for young people, is practically nonexistent. Prior to 1978 there were no books on the subject in the juvenile area, either fiction or non-fiction. One mediocre series on minorities in America included a brief reference to the genocide in its volume on the Armenians. **The World Book Encyclopedia** has five lines on the genocide under Armenia, and one line under genocide; the **New Book of Knowledge**, under Armenia, says only, "see Union of Socialist Soviet Republics." The Armenian Genocide is mentioned in few history textbooks; the text that has the most material on the Holocaust has less than two pages about the Armenians.

The two juvenile titles listed here, published in 1978 and 1979 respectively, are the first available for children on this subject. The Bedoukian book was originally published in England as an adult title; the Kherdian book, however, was an American Library Association Honor Book in 1979, and is a worthy title to be the first true children's book about the Armenian Genocide.

For additional materials on the Armenian Genocide, contact one of the following:

National Association for Armenian Studies and Research, Inc.
175 Mt. Auburn Street, Cambridge, MA 02138   (617) 497-6713
    Zoryan Institute
5 Fayerweather Street, Cambridge, MA 02138   (617) 497-6713
    Armenian Assembly
122 "C" Street, Washington, DC 20001

In adult literature, the field is somewhat broader, but it still has nowhere near the scope of Holocaust literature. There is not really a literature of the Armenian Genocide as there is of the Holocaust. Not only are the books fewer in number, but they are more difficult to find. Few of them are published by major publishing houses; some are published privately, some by Armenian organizations—they are not readily available in local bookstores and libraries. There is also a notable lack of fiction; the one major novel, **The Forty Days of Musa Dagh,** has been out of print for years. For these reasons, this portion of the bibliography is neither as comprehensive nor as selective as that on the literature of the Holocaust.

Children's Books

Bedoukian, Kerop   **Some of Us Survived**
Farrar, Straus & Giroux, 1978
Basically, this is the American edition of a book originally published in England as **The Urchin.** The English edition was published as an adult book; the only changes in the American edition are in format and editing—shorter paragraphs, spelling and punctuation changes, and occasional rewordings. The format is both more attractive and more readable than the English version. The first part of the book describes the author's experiences during a deportation march which began in 1915. The family was resettled, first at Birejek, then at Aleppo. They finally went to Constantinople and when the massacres resumed, left there for Bulgaria, and eventually Canada. This work documents the effects of the Turkish onslaught on one family, seen through the eyes of a child. The description of the march includes some graphic accounts of atrocity.

Kherdian, David   **The Road From Home: The Story of an Armenian Girl**
Greenwillow (Morrow), 1979
David Kherdian is the author of several volumes of poetry for both children and adults. Here he has written the story of his mother's childhood. This is not a formal biography, but a first-person narrative, one of those books that falls in the crack between biography and fictionalized history, fictionalized only in the sense that conversations and trivia are included to make the book more readable—the historical and biographical information is all authentic. Kherdian's mother was Veron Dumehjian, born in 1907 in Turkey, into a prosperous Armenian family. The book tells her life story from the early years to the age of 16, when she left for the United States as a "mail-order bride." A historical introduction explains the background of the Armenian situation in Turkey, and the biographical account includes the years of slaughter and deportations, when Veron lost both parents and

siblings. It is a well-written, moving account of a part of history seldom dealt with in children's literature. A sequel, **Finding Home** (Greenwillow, 1981), tells of Veron Dumehjian's life in America, and describes the birth of the Armenian community in Racine, Wisconsin.

Topalian, Naomi   **Dust to Destiny**
            Baikar Publications, 1986   Available from the author: 46 Circle Road, Lexington, MA 02173
            Taman Zarhoui was born in 1892 in Turkish Armenia; her story is written by her daughter in the first person, as her mother originally told it to her. The story really begins in 1895, with the Turkish massacre of Armenians in Marash; Taman is 3, and loses her mother and her 18-month-old sister at this time. She is raised in a German orphanage, and has become a teacher by the onset of World War I, and a new wave of atrocity. She later marries and settles in Lebanon, where she remains until she comes to the United States at the age of 78. Her life seemed to be filled with hardship and loss, both due to and apart from the massacres, but her strength, courage, and spirit are an inspiration. Unlike most such stories, it has a happy ending -- Taman Zarhoui Getsoyan died at the age of 92, surrounded by her children, grandchildren, and great grand-children. The book is only a little more than 100 pagees long, and the reading level would make it appropriate for most junior high students.

Adult Books

Alamudden, Ida   **Papa Kuenzler and the Armenians**
            Heinemann, 1970
            Jacob Kuenzler was a Swiss who joined a German mission in Turkey toward the end of the 19th century and served there for 25 years, years that included the Armenian massacres. During those years he devoted himself to the care of the victims. In the early twenties he began working for the Near East Relief Organization, evacuating Armenians from Turkey. This account of his life and work was written by his daughter. It is clear, informal and readable, a book that could be read by many young people.

Arlen, Michael   **Passage to Ararat**
            Farrar, Straus & Giroux, 1975 (paper, Ballantine)
            Arlen's father was Armenian, but he seldom spoke of his country or his people. In order to discover his own roots, the author set out to learn what it meant to be Armenian. He read Armenian history, travelled to the land that once was Armenia, and talked with people of Armenian extraction. Gradually, he pieced together what seemed to be the forgotten story of the Armenian Genocide. The

result is an autobiography which personalizes the fate of an entire people and presents a little-known period of history in a highly readable manner for both students and teachers.

Armenian Genocide: Facts and Documents Introduction by Yves Ternon
St. Vartan Press, 1984
The chronology of the main events of the genocide are provided here, along with a brief historical outline. Other documents pertain to international law, the Turkish position, and the correction of myths and misleading information disseminated by the Turkish government. One chapter deals with the position of the German government and its failure to prevent the massacres.

Aslanian, H. Jack   **Fixed Movements: A Portion From Our Past**
Strawberry Hill Press
A novel about a romantic young man who visits his homeland with other Americans of Armenian origin in this tale about immigrants in transition and in transit, returning to their home place to confront, often painfully, their own pasts.

Aved, Thomas G.   **Toomas, the Little Armenian Boy: Childhood Reminiscence of Turkish-Armenia**
Pioneer Publishing Co., 1979
Toomas and his family lived in Istanbul for several years following the massacres. The experiences of his childhood during those tumultuous years is related here, told by the author in the third person.

Bardakjian, Kevork B.   **Hitler and the Armenian Genocide**
Zoryan Institute for Contemporary Armenian Research and Documentation, Inc., 1985
Scholars have argued that the absence of justice in the Armenian genocide encouraged Hitler to believe that he would not be held responsible for his own crimes against humanity. Dr. Bardakjian has undertaken the most extensive research to date on Hitler's statement to his generals on the eve of the invasion of Poland, "Who remembers now the extermination of the Armenians?" He has traced the source of the document, the circumstances of its publication, and compared the three existing versions. He also explores the reasons why this document was never entered as evidence at the Nuremberg Tribunal.

Bey, Naim   **Memoirs of Naim Bey**   Translated by Aram Andonian
Armenian Historical Research Association, 1965
This collection of documents and telegrams reveals the communication between Talaat Pasha and the deportation officials at Aleppo. Naim Bey was head of the General Deportation Committee of Aleppo in 1915, and the documents

collected in this book were given by him to an Armenian named Aram Andonian, who translated them into English. This book includes some photocopies of original telegrams. Much of this material was excerpted for the Facing History and Ourselves curriculum.

Boyajian, Dickran H.   **Armenia: The Case for a Forgotten Genocide**
     Educational Book Crafters, 1972
     This is a collection of many documents used to support Armenian territorial claims. It includes the full text of the Harbord Report, the Congressional Record of the American Military Mission to Armenia. Portions of this Report have been taken out of context and used by Turkish historians to support their claim that relations between Turks and Armenians have always been harmonious.

Bryce, Viscount **The Treatment of Armenians in the Ottoman Empire 1915-1916**
     Beirut, Lebanon, 1916
     Although this is a massive collection of eyewitness accounts, it includes only a portion of the actual deportations and deaths which eliminated entire Armenian communities. The largest section documents "neutral eyewitnesses passing through or living temporarily in Turkey." Other sections include testimony of "native Christians" and "Germans in Turkey." Most of the selections are brief and could be used with students.

Case of Soghomon Tehlirian (Armenian Political Trials -- Proceedings) Translated by V. Yeghiayan
     Published by ARF Varantian Gomideh, Los Angeles, CA, 1985
     Tehlirian was a survivor of the genocide of the Armenians in 1915-1917. In 1921, he assissinated Talaat Pasha, Minster of the Interior and mastermind of the genocide. Talaat had fled to Germany for refuge, and it was in Berlin that Tehlirian found and killed him. The book documents the proceedings of his trial.

Crime of Silence -- The Armenian Genocide: The Permanent People's Tribunal Preface by Vidal Naguet
     Zed Books, London, 1985
     The Permanent People's Tribunal held a special hearing in Paris in 1985 to commemorate the 70th anniversary of the Armenian massacre. This volume presents the evidence and papers delivered at the Tribunal's hearings, as well as its verdict. It includes material on the official Turkish denial, German eyewitness reports, the ideology of the Young Turk Movement, and a report of the genocide itself.

Genocide of the Armenian People

El-Ghusein, Fa'iz **Martyred Armenia**
Tankian Publishing Corp., 1975
This provides a Bedouin's eyewitness account of Armenian massacres, and the writing contains much gruesome horror. As the author states, "The purpose of this book is to defend the faith of Islam against the charge of fanaticism, which will be brought against it by Europeans" once the world becomes aware of the massacres.

Genocide: Crime Against Humanity -- Essays & Documents
Armenian Review, Watertown, MA Vol 37, #1, Spring, 1984
This entire issue of the Armenian Review is devoted to the history and documentation of the Armenian genocide. It includes thirty documents from State Department files, eyewitness accounts from American and European missionaries. It also contains articles written on major aspects of documentation found in the U.S. archives.

Gibbons, Harbert Adams **Blackest Page of Modern History: Events in Armenia**
Tankian Publishing Corp., 1975
From 1908 to 1913, the author traveled through Europe, Asia, and Turkey, and became acquainted with men who guided the destinies of the Ottoman Empire. In those five years, he witnessed events that changed the hope of generations into despair and dissolution. He spent most of his time in Constantinople, and writes of the events he witnessed there.

Hartunian, Abraham H. **Neither to Laugh Nor to Weep: A Memoir of the Armenian Genocide** Translated by Vartan Hartunian
Beacon Press, 1968; 2nd edition, Armenian Heritage Press 1986
This is the story of an Armenian Protestant pastor who survived the massacres and escaped to the United States. It is translated by the author's son. The book is divided chronologically into three parts: part I, 1912-1914— background on the author's youth and the beginnings of political unrest; Part II, 1914-1918— the First World War and the worst period of Armenian slaughter; and Part III, 1919-1922—deportations, more massacres, world intervention (or the lack of), and, finally, escape. A great deal of history is included in this autobiographical account. The revised edition contains introductory essays by Marjorie Housepian Dobkin and the late Ambassador Henry Morgenthau.

Highgas, Dirouhi Kouymjian **Refugee Girl**
Baikar Publications
The autobiographical account of an Armenian girl born in Konia, southern Turkey, her carefree early life, the Turkish deportations, and her courageous struggle to save her loved ones. The account ends with the author's arrival in the United States in 1929.

80

Housepian, Marjorie   **Unremembered Genocide (A Commentary Report)**
Commentary Magazine, Vol. 42, Sept., 1966
The history of the Armenian prople, their role in the Ottoman Empire, and the Turkish policies toward them are all covered, as well as the massacres themselves, and Henry Morganthau's role as ambassador to Turkey during the first year of the massacres. The Turkish policy of denial is discussed, including the present day policy.

Housepian, Marjorie   **Smyrna 1922: The Destruction of a City**
Faber, 1972
The author has provided a detailed scholarly account of events in Smyrna between the end of the First World War and the rise of the Turkish nationalists. Part of the importance of this book is in its documentation of the fact that the destruction and massacres continued well after the end of World War I; many of those who are aware that the Armenian Genocide happened at all, think that it was an event that took place only around 1915.

Hovannisian, Richard G., editor   **Armenian Genocide in Perspective**
Tranasction Books, 1986
A compilation of essays written by specialists in several disciplines, this work examines the Armenian genocide from the perspecitves of history, politics, ethics, religion, literarture, sociology, and psychology. It explores the implications of denial and rationalization, and the impact of the Armenian genocide on the world during and after World War I. This anthology not only makes a significant contribution to the study of the Armenian genocide, but serves as an excellent introduction to the study of genocide in general. These essays were originally presented at the 1982 Conference on the Holocaust and Genocide in Tel Aviv.

Hovannisian, Richard G.   **Armenia on the Road to Independence**
University of California Press, 1967
The author states in his introduction that the "object of this study is to present and analyze the numerous complex factors that led to the establishment of an Armenian government for the first time in more than five hundred years." The book begins with a look at historic Armenia, Russian Armenia and Turkish Armenia; it then covers the years of World War I and the Bolshevik Revolution. Over half the book, however, concentrates on the year 1918, as the title indicates. Based largely on documents in the National Archives, the book is well documented, including over 50 pages of notes and an unannotated bibliography of over 25 pages. The author has also written a full history of the Armenian Republic.

Kerr, Stanley E.   **The Lions of Marash: Personal Experiences—American Near Relief 1919-1922**
SUNY Press, 1973
Kerr's account of the French evacuation of Marash and the subsequent victory of the Turkish Nationalist troops is written with respect for all groups caught in the conflict. He concentrates on the decisions that the Armenians, the American Relief Team, the Turkish Muslim citizens, Nationalist troops, and the French Army all had to make during the block-to-block struggle for survival. Excerpts could be used with students.

Kloian, Diran, comp. & ed.   **The Armenian Genocide - First 20th Century Holocaust: The Events in Turkish Armenia (1914- 1916) as Reported in the New York Times and Various Periodicals of the Time with Selected Entries to 1922**
Armenian Commemorative Committee, 1980
The title of this work is self-explanatory; it is simply a compilation of original source material. It is, however, the result of much research, and an invaluable tool in the study of the Armenian Genocide.

Lang, David Marshall   **The Armenians: A People in Exile**
Allen & Unwin, 1981
Lang is Professor of Caucasian Studies at SOAS, University of London; from 1944 to 1946 he was British Vice- Consul at Tabriz, Persian Azerbaijan. This is his third book about Armenia and the Armenians. This volume deals with the Armenian diaspora, some six and a half million Armenians scattered throughout the world, and the persecutions of the Armenians at the hands of the Turks from 1895 to 1922. In addition, he includes chapters on such topics as the Armenians in business, literature, music, and art. He discusses their contributions to world culture, and general information about their own culture and way of life.

Morgenthau, Henry   **Ambassador Morgenthau's Story**
New Age Publishers, 1975
Henry Morgenthau was the United States Ambassador to Turkey from 1913 to 1916. This book was first published in 1919; in it the ambassador chronicles the war years, with the emphasis on the role of the German government in Turkey. He also provides a first-hand account of the destruction of the Armenians. He describes his own attempts, as representative of the American government, to intervene on behalf of the Armenian people, and the Turkish response to his efforts.

Nalbandian, Louise Z.   **The Armenian Revolutionary Movement: The Development of Armenian Political Parties Through the Nineteenth Century**
University of California Press, 1963
This book has been an important source for both Armenian and Turkish scholars. The Turkish government claims that the Armenian Revolutionary Parties of the late nineteenth century represented the leadership and support of Armenian communities in Eastern Turkey, and therefore, for security reasons, all Armenians had to be relocated. Armenian scholars claim that the Revolutionary Parties represented only a fringe element and did not have widespread support. The author indicates that the role and input of Armenian revolutionaries cannot be compared to the force and impact of Arabs during the Arab revolt against the Ottoman Empire in 1916.

Sachar, Howard M.   **The Emergence of the Middle East 1914- 1924**
Knopf, 1969
In this general history of the Middle East, the author devotes one chapter to the Armenian Genocide. He provides a scholarly account that has been cited by some historians for inaccuracies, but is still the most concise and readable account to use with students. It is primarily focused on military strategy.

Samelian, Varaz   **A History of Armenia and My Life**
By the Author, 1978
A brief history of Armenia is presented in words and pictures at the beginning of this book. The rest is an autobiography of the author, with the emphasis placed on his life as a Russian soldier in the Second World War, which included time spent in a German prison camp. It concludes with a brief account of his life in California after the war. The entire text is interspersed with reproductions of art works done by the author, striking portrayals of the effects of war. He is one of the few whose lives included both the Armenian Genocide and the Nazi Holocaust.

Shipley, Alice M.   **We Walked, Then Ran**
A.M. Shipley, Phoenix, AZ, 1983
Alice Muggerditchian's father was an interpreter in the diplomatic service of the British government from 1914 to 1921. Alice was nine years old when she, with her mother and siblings, left the comforts of the Diplomatic House to go into hiding in Turkey. They escaped to Russia -- right in the middle of the Bolshevik Revoluiton. They eventually reached the United States, where Alice has recorded the story of their struggles, and their survival.

Sanjian, Avedis K.   **The Armenian Communities in Syria Under Ottoman Dominion**
Harvard University Press, 1965
This is a study of the social and economic institutions of Armenian communities in Syria. Although it is a regional study, it offers insights into the Armenian community in general. Chapter Two explains the millet, a system of dividing communities into religious, rather than national or racial, units; in the millet, each community was allowed to retain its own civil laws. Sanjian describes at length the Armenian millet—how the community was run and its internal power struggles.

Shiragian, Arshavir   **The Legacy: Memoirs of an Armenian Patriot**
Hairenik Press, 1976
The author began his career as a young gun smuggler in Constantinople during the First World War. After the war, when it became clear that the Allies did not intend to punish the perpetrators of the Armenian Genocide, Shiragian became part of an organization dedicated to the discovery and execution of Turkish war criminals. His memoirs describe his terrorist activity, including the political assassination of Turks by his hand in Rome and Berlin, and his subsequent escape to the United States. This is a fast- paced adventure story rather than a formal history. Its major theme is revenge and a rationale for terrorism.

Suajian, Stephen G.   **Trip to Historic Armenia**
GreenHill, 1977
The focus of this Armenian history is on Turkish-Armenian relations, highlighting both Armenian and Middle Eastern history. It includes memoirs of the massacres and the First World War, as well as description of the author's trip through historic Armenia and Eastern Turkey. His own extensive research and personal knowledge is supplemented with numerous eyewitness accounts.

Toynbee, Arnold J.   **Armenian Atrocities -- The Murder of a Nation**
Tankian Publishing Corp., 1975
Toynbee looks with the eye of an historian at Armenia and its people before the Genocide, and at the motivation of the Turkish leaders who initiated the genocide. He also examines the 1915 massacres -- the plans, the massacres themselves, and the toll of destruction. His sources include personal depositions and letters, and testimonies from missionaries; he ends with a discussion of the German attitude toward the Armenian genocide.

Toynbee, Arnold   **The Murderous Tyranny of the Turks**
Tankian Publishing Co., 1975
This is a reprint of a pamphlet originally published in Great Britain in 1917, chiefly of interest because of the fame of its author. Toynbee's aim is to justify the Allied plans to eliminate Turkey from Europe at the end of the war, by explaining "the murderous tyranny of the Turks both historically and at the time of the writing." It includes a capsulized history of the Turkish invasions in both Europe and Asia Minor.

Walker, Christopher J.   **Armenia: The Survival of a Nation**
St. Martin's Press, 1980
In this history of modern Armenia, Walker looks at the events that preceded the 1915 massacres, especially at the role of Great Britain and Russia, what they did and what they failed to do. He covers the deportations and massacres that occurred in 1915, and related the Armenians' attempt to create a state of their own near the end of the First World War. The concluding chapter deals with events since 1921, when the Caucasian border was fixed. He also includes brief biographies of major Armenian political, military and literary figures. The prologue is called "Theatre of Perpetual War," an all-too-appropriate description of modern Armenia.

Werfel, Franz   **The Forty Days of Musa Dagh**
Viking, 1934
The author of this 800-page novel (translated from German to English) states in a note at the beginning of the book that he was inspired to write it after seeing a group of refugees in Damascus in 1929. The novel is the story of one group of Armenian villagers and their struggle to resist the Turks. Musa Dagh means "Mountain of Moses"; it was at the summit of this mountain that Armenians from seven surrounding villages took their final stand against the Turkish Army, and they survived there for forty days until rescued by a French warship. Ironically, Werfel himself, the author of what is to date the only major novel of the Armenian Genocide, was forced to flee his Austrian home when Austria was invaded by the Nazis.

Choosing To Participate

Choosing to participate is an outgrowth of Facing History's work with issues of justice and the individual's responsibility to society. We have been reading, thinking and piloting lessons about how people in American history and in today's society choose to become involved—in community work, in human service, in social activism and in other kinds of voluntary and nonprofit activity. We believe it is important for students to learn more about the potential for individuals and groups to create change, from shaping the direction of society at large to improving the most immediate circumstances of life. This annotated bibliography of our reading reflects where we have looked so far for ideas, knowledge and guidance as we have approached a broad subject. We hope our work contributes to and fuels interest in a growing field of study.

Our initial research into voluntary activity and community participation led us to new ways of considering vital issues— such as the nature of individual responsibility in a democratic society, motivations to care and act for others, and the possibilities for creating positive social change. These concerns have always been central to Facing History's work about twentieth-century genocide. Responses of students suggest that learning about abuses of power stimulates a desire to find some models and methods of prevention. Yet students are usually unsure of where to look for avenues of participation that can improve our society.

The following bibliography describes some of the books that helped us explore the broad themes of the morality and values of community and self. It also lists some of the more accessible books that helped us in our research of nonprofit activity, voluntarism and youth participation. A more extensive annotated listing is available from the Resource Center.

Arendt, Hannah   **On Revolution**
         Viking Press, 1963
         Arendt draws distinctions between liberation and freedom with implica-
tions for the participation of citizens in a democracy. Arendt emphasizes that
liberation restores rights that were lost. It is liberation from, while freedom is a
more positive quality, it is freedom to. Liberty is a right while freedom is what
people choose when they become involved in collective society. America's great
contribution to the world was not the American Revolution; 1776 was supplanted
in the world's imagination by the French Revolution as the model for sudden
political change, which contributed to the dominant Hegelian understanding that
humans ride torrents of inevitable historical forces without ultimate power to
influence the course of events. Instead, the great American development was the
movement of a free people beyond the mass poverty of European experience. It
remains for us to transcend our desires for private wealth and liberty to seek the
freedom of participating in the decisions of society as a whole. Arendt's thinking is
important for Daniel Yankelovich, who sees the American potential for advancing
civilization in her terms.

Barber, Benjamin   **Strong Democracy: Participatory Politics for a New Age**
         University of California Press, 1984
         Barber recasts the tension between liberty and democracy. While liberties
are essential to democracy, a longstanding fear of democracy's champions and
critics is that a democratic majority may infringe on minority rights. Barber
reverses the charge that democracy is a danger to liberty, claiming that our
understanding and practice of liberty has limited our practice of democracy. Our
system of representative democracy impedes real participation and citizenship.
Liberal democracy fails because it tries to adapt pure democracy, where all people
rule on all matters, to a mass scale, and results in weak democracy, where a very
small number of people are entrusted with our political decisions. Barber proposes
that democracy can become strong if all citizens have an active role in self-
government in some public matters some of the time. Barber extensively analyzes
and attacks different philosophical and psychological underpinnings that support
the pessimistic view of democracy, yet he realistically recognizes that a strong
democracy of active citizenship can only be built in the context of our current
representative institutions.

Bellah, Robert, Richard Madsen, William Sullivan, Ann Swidler and Steven Tipton
Habits of the Heart: Individualism and Commitment in American Life
University of California Press, 1985

Four sociologists and a philosopher analyze how Americans struggle to value both the individual and the community in a society that is dominated and threatened by individualistic thinking. Beneath our language of individualism we retain desires for community that we cannot readily articulate. In the utilitarian thinking of therapy and the popular psychology of the middle class, we tend to value commitments as long as they fulfill our hopes for reward and personal expression, but our ability has declined to see a moral aspect to these commitments that would more solidly link us to others. Commitments to family and community persist but suffer from our inability to articulate the value of efforts contributing beyond the self. Our traditions of religious community and civic responsibility offer, with imperfections, partial alternatives to individualism, but their power is currently hampered by our tendency to view such involvement only in terms of self-satisfaction and self-interest. The authors stress a need for a new moral discourse that will help us to think about balancing individual and social needs.

Bremner, Robert H.   **American Philanthropy** (University of Chicago History of American Civilization series)
University of Chicago Press, 1960

Bremner's book is a very readable starting point for an understanding of the evolution of American efforts to address poverty and other social problems. The history shows how different social philosophies and historical circumstances have influenced the development of voluntary poverty relief, social work and social services, of foundations, and of government programs that in the twentieth century subordinated many private efforts. Bremner clearly traces the changing values about charity and about class of voluntary and private institutions and government programs.

Evans, Sara M., and Harry C. Boyte   **Free Spaces: The Sources of Democratic Change in America**
Harper & Row, 1986

Evans and Boyte argue that democracy is created and nurtured in the institutions of service and advocacy that lie in between the realms of private life and the fully public life of government institutions. In the "free spaces" of voluntary association and organization, people find opportunities to realize the values of equality and self-government that underlie democracy and develop the skills of organization, debate and group action that are required for democracy to work. Evans and Boyte devote much of the book to case studies of organizations in the civil rights, labor, populist and women's movements, including Southern churches, the Knights of Labor, the Women's Christian Temperance Union, and many modern descendants to demonstrate how the values and skills of democracy are built over time through people's shared energy and work. Evans and Boyte strongly suggest that American traditions of voluntary association hold much promise for efforts to create a more democratic society.

Kohler, Mary Conway   **Young People Learning to Care: Making a Difference Through Youth Participation**
Seabury Press, 1983
Kohler's lifetime involvement with adolescents has led her to see great potential in providing young people with opportunities to care for others. Kohler believes that adolescents have a strong need to believe in themselves that is thwarted by the lack of opportunities to demonstrate care actively. Children who are excessively indulged or ignored can end up feeling that they are the only ones who matter; without positive experiences to develop a sense of interdependence with others, adolescents will have harder times learning how to balance independence and dependence on others. Kohler believes youth participation must provide challenges and responsibilities of real decision-making in helping to meet genuine needs.

MacIntyre, Alastair   **After Virtue**
University of Notre Dame Press, 1981
A Scottish philosopher describes the fragmentation of Western civilization's collective sense of morality over the past several centuries. The book seeks to explain why so many contemporary moral arguments seem unresolvable and how morality has fallen from a social enterprise to a matter of personal taste. By contrasting modern versions of morality with earlier ones, MacIntyre develops a general understanding of morality as a continuous dialogue about the traditions of practices and customs within a community. **After Virtue** is challenging and engaging, even for the philosophically untutored, and an excellent preparation for **Habits of the Heart**, which draws on MacIntyre in substantial ways.

Mathews, David   **"Civic Intelligence"**
Social Education, November/December 1985 (Vol. 49, No. 8), pp. 678-681
Mathews makes a strong argument for the renewal of civic education as a central goal for schools. He suggests that "civic intelligence" is composed of specific skills that can be taught in the classroom. For Mathews, civic intelligence involves the understanding of connectedness to society, an appreciation of how others see a situation and a tolerance for disagreement. Civic skills of listening, of dialogue and of discriminating between facts and values are both the most basic of tools needed for participating in a democracy and among the most essential intellectual skills that teachers have long hoped to encourage in students. Renewed

attention to these basics of critical thinking can be supported by the goal of developing students' civic intelligence.

Payton, Robert L.   **Major Challenges to Philanthropy** (a discussion paper prepared for the 1984 annual meeting of Independent Sector)
Independent Sector, 1984
    Payton casts a wide net of questions and dilemmas about nonprofit activity: What is the purpose of philanthropy? Should philanthropy exclude compassion and relief efforts to focus on more long-term solutions that address underlying problems? How do mercy and justice conflict? Does voluntary aid to the poor preclude their rights to assistance? Payton avoids answering all his questions, instead offering intellectual and historical backgrounds that challenge and help us to ask them of ourselves. Although Payton is an ardent proponent of the voluntary sector, he is willing to consider some of its most fundamental criticisms.

Peavey, Fran   **Heart Politics**
New Society Publishers, 1986
    Fran Peavey, a teacher and human rights activist, expands our ideas about creating change. With humor and compassion she relates her own stories of community work, which range from her individual "American Willing To Listen" project, a global search for fresh perspective, to a group effort to establish and maintain a park that is run by and for the down-and-out of San Francisco. Peavey emphasizes the importance of informed participation; her greatest skill perhaps lies in listening, working diligently to understand the position and values not only of people in need but also of people on the other side of political struggles. Through deeper knowledge of both allies and opponents, our vision widens for possibilities of service, advocacy and compromise. The author's portraits offer tenacious reminders of the resilience of the human spirit. "How will we learn to respect our untouchables?" Fran Peavey asks. "And how will we create a context where they can respect themselves?"

Yankelovich, Daniel   **New Rules: Searching for Self-Fulfillment in a World Turned Upside Down**
Random House, 1981
Yankelovich uses survey statistics and descriptive portraits to describe fundamental changes in American values over the past several decades. He explores the relationship between changes in values to changes in our economy, and outlines the emergence of a new ethic of commitment. Although the changes in values of the past two decades involved recognizing the limits of adhering too much to the status quo of work and family, new choices of career and personal relationships have not been easy, especially in a less expansive economy. At the same time, the excessive orientation toward satisfying the needs of self have impoverished efforts to find more roundly satisfying lives. Although Americans' sensitivity toward the problems of marginal members of our society seems currently weakened, much potential exists in the development of the nascent ethic of commitment. Yankelovich sees in the new ethic a potential to fulfill Arendt's hopes for revolution that will move from simple liberty to real cultural and political freedom, where freedom involves not simply liberation *from* poverty and oppression but the richer freedom to share the power of making social choices.

Appendix A

Basic Reading Lists

The following lists have been designed both to include the most significant books, and to present a wide range of views of the Holocaust. Full annotations of these titles can be found in the main body of the bibliography.

Junior High

Ablells, Chana   **Children We Remember**   Graphic black-and white photographs present a striking glimpse of children, from pre-war scenes to the Nazi takeover.

Atkinson, Linda   **In Kindling Flame**   Biography of Hannah Senesh, Jewish resistance fighter, combined with relevant history.

Forman, James   **Ceremonies of Innocence**   Fictionalized story of Hans and Sophie Scholl, members of the German White Rose student resistance movement.

Forman, James   **The Survivor**   Chronicle of a Jewish Dutch boy, from the occupation to Auschwitz and back to Holland, the only surviving member of his family.

Isaacman, Clara   **Clara's Story**   Clara's autobiography parallels Anne Frank's story in many ways, but includes more historical perspective.

Koehn, Ilse   **Mischling, Second Degree**   True story of a German girl who is declared Jewish by the Nuremberg laws because she had a Jewish grandparent.

Meltzer, Milton   **Never To Forget**   History of the Holocaust, focusing on the destruction and resistance of the Jews.

Sender, Ruth Minsky   **The Cage**   The author, a Polish Jew, dramatically describes her experiences from the ghetto to Auschwitz, and to a labor camp.

Switzer, Ellen   **How Democracy Failed**   Germans in the '70s look back on their memories, as teen-agers in Nazi Germany.

von Staden, Wendelgard **Darkness Over the Valley**   Memories of a German girl, caught up in the Nazi movement, until she begins to see its evils.

High School

Bauer, Yehuda   **History of the Holocaust**   A detailed chronicle of Holocaust events, by country, is preceded by a study of the historical background of Nazism, antisemitism, Jewish life, and German-Jewish relations.

Dumbach, Annette E.   **Shattering the German Night**   Well researched history of the White Rose movement, and portraits of its leaders.

Eisner, Jack   **The Survivor**   Autobiographical account of a teen-age ghetto fighter.

Gies, Meip   **Anne Frank Remembered**   The woman who helped hide the Frank family adds important historical perspective to the diary.

Hart, Kitty   **Return To Auschwitz**   After making a TV documentary of the same title, Kitty recalls the events that led her to Auschwitz and the trauma of her return.

Jackson, Livia E.   **Elli: Coming of Age in the Holocaust**   Detailed account of life in the camps from the perspective of an adolescent girl.

Korschunow, Irfma   **Night in Distant Motion**   Novel about a German girl who is a loyal Nazi until she falls in love with a Polish prisoner.

Leitner, Isabella   **Fragments of Isabella**   Eloquent account of personal experiences in Auschwitz, and the legacy of hope left by her mother.

Mayer, Milton   **They Thought They Were Free**   Germans after the war discuss what the Nazi had been and how he got that way.

Oberski, Jona   **Childhood**   Devastating account of the Holocaust as seen through the eyes of a very young child.

Ramati, Alexander   **And the Violins Stopped Playing**   Novel based on the experiences of a teen-age Gypsy boy, from Poland to Auschwitz, and back.

Suhl, Yuri   **They Fought Back**   Anthology of accounts of Jewish resistance, by historians, witnesses, and survivors.

Wiesel, Elie   **Night**   Memoir of the author's experiences from Hungary to Auschwitz, masterfully told by the best known of Holocaust writers.

Appendix A

Adult

Borowski, Tadeusz   **This Way to the Gas, Ladies and Gentlemen**   A collection of remarkable short stories set in the camps, stories that deal with moral issues and personal feelings, rather than events.

Delbo, Charlotte   **None of Us Will Return**   In poetic prose, the author takes the reader, not inside the camp, but inside the captive; her visual images are unsurpassed.

Dobroszycki, Lucjan   **Chronicle of the Lodz Ghetto**   Selections from original documents written by the archivists of the Lodz ghetto, introduced and edited by its only survivor.

Dumbach, Annette E.   **Shattering the German Night**   Well-researched history of the White Rose movement, and portraits of the leaders of this German student resistance group.

Gilbert, Martin   **The Holocaust**   A definitive work, more than 800 pages of historical research and personal accounts; well-indexed — good reference tool, as well as a readable history.

Kamenetsky, Christa   **Children's Literature in Hitler's Germany**   History of the Nazi attempt to control children's reading, from selection and adaptation of materials to control of libraries and publishers.

Kuznetsov, Anatoli   **Babi Yar**   History merges with autobiography in this account of the German invasion of Kiev and its re-capture by the Russians, including eyewitness accounts of the atrocities committed at the ravine known as Babi Yar.

Langer, Lawrence   **Death and The Age of Atrocity**   From individual death to death by atrocity, Langer uses modern writers to illustrate how modern atrocities like the Holocaust have altered conceptions of life, death, and humanity.

Leitner, Isabella   **Fragments of Isabella**   Eloquent account of the author's experiences in Auschwitz, and the legacy of hope, love and faith left by her mother.

Levi, Primo   **Survival in Auschwitz**   Documentary evidence of life in Auschwitz in terms of both outward activities and inward reactions, brilliantly depicted by an Italian Jew who was in Auschwitz at the time of the liberation.

Holocaust and Human Behavior Bibliography

Mayer, Milton   **They Thought They Were Free**   Interviews with
Germans after the war to learn what the Nazi had been and how he got that
way.

Ramati, Alexander   **And the Violins Stopped Playing**   Novel based on the
experiences of a teen-age Gypsy boy, from Poland to Auschwitz, and
back.

Sereny, Gita   **Into That Darkness**   In interviewing Franz Stangl in
prison in 1971, Ms. Sereny provides what is probably the best available
portrait of a Nazi, both in terms of outward actions and inner reactions.

Suhl, Yuri   **They Fought Back**   Anthology of accounts of Jewish
resistance, by historians, witnesses, and survivors.

Wiesel, Elie   **Night**   Memoir of the author's experiences from
Hungary to Auschwitz, masterfully told by the best known of Holocaust
writers.

Ziemer, Gregor   **Education for Death**   The author describes in detail
the Nazi educational system, based on personal visits to the school during
the thirties.

Appendix B

Myth vs. Reality: Literature As History

Many of the books mentioned in the overview are fiction, as are many of those on the following lists. Fiction is an extremely effective way of giving a personal touch to history; the experiences of one person or family are much easier to identify with than a straight recitation of facts and figures, especially for children. Fiction, however, can be used to convey reality or to perpetuate myth. The danger in most children's fiction is the authors' tendencies to gloss over the harsh aspects of an event and emphasize more positive things — the victories and the heroes, rather than the defeats and the victims.

Take, for example, Marie McSwigan's book, **Snow Treasure**, originally published in 1942, during the war, and still popular with children today. The basis of the story is factual, the story of the smuggling of Norway's gold out of the country after the Nazi invasion. The children take the gold out on their sleds, right under the Nazi's eyes, and, as the story is written, it is a wonderful adventure. The children treat the whole thing as a game, swearing never to tell even if tortured, with the author using phrases such as "Michael's eyes shone with excitement." Even when one of the boys is captured, it seems only to set the scene for a daring rescue and escape.

Contrast this with the two boys in Arnost Lustig's **Darkness Casts No Shadows**, a novel written for adults. There may be no factual basis for this story at all, but it conveys a sense of reality that the other book, though based on solid facts, fails to do. Here are children who struggle painstakingly through a forest for hours, without food or water, only to find they have travelled in a circle and are back where they started. Here is a child who remembers his father's death in the concentration camp, and remembers hoping that his mother had died too, that he would not see her "among those frail, naked, barefoot women, picking their way through the October mud and stones and snow..." This child describes his terrible feeling of loneliness and desperation as "feeling you're in your own way, just by being alive..."

A book like this may be fiction, but it is still reality, whereas a book like **Snow Treasure**, though based on fact, is the perpetration of a myth, or perhaps a fairy tale, that begins "once upon a time" and ends "happily ever after." Fortunately, not all children's books are as blatantly romanticized as this one, but neither do many of them truthfully present reality. They present only a small piece of the picture, usually one of the more pleasant pieces; their only value as history is to broaden the perspectives of a reader who already has some background knowledge of the historical facts. Without this background, they would present only a distorted view; with it, they can widen the scope of a reader's knowledge.

No attempt will be made here to describe the plots of individual books; that information is available in other sources. Neither are individual annotations needed in most cases; within a given category, the titles generally have the same strengths or weaknesses. Individual titles are mentioned only when they differ in some significant respect from others in the same category. Several of the titles are personal narratives, classified as non-fiction in some libraries, but the criteria for historical fiction should also be applied to autobiography. For the purpose of this bibliography, only books relating to the period of the second World War and the Holocaust are included, although the same principles would hold true of all historical fiction.

Stories of Escape or Hiding

Escape stories always make good reading, and all of these are well-written; without the background provided by the Meltzer book, however, they simply do not tell the story. The realities of what the Jews are running from are not there, in many cases because the story is told from a child's point of view, and the child did not really understand what was happening. The reader with the proper historical background can learn much by seeing events through the eyes of a child, but these books have limitations.

Hautzig	**The Endless Steppe: Growing Up in Siberia**
Holm	**North to Freedom**
Kerr	**When Hitler Stole Pink Rabbit**
Levitin	**Journey to America**
Sachs	**A Pocketful of Seeds**
Serraillier	**The Silver Sword**
Sommerfelt	**Miriam**
Wojciechowska	**Till the Break of Day**

Appendix B

Stories of The Resistance

These are the books that should be used with the most caution and looked at with the most critical eye. They are glorious adventure stories, and the war was an exciting, almost exhilarating time to be alive. Many of them could have been written about any war — the war is merely a good setting for a story. The facts are frequently incidental; the Second World War was a period of history that provides an excellent background for an adventure story. It creates wonderful heroes, fighting valiantly to save the "poor Jew", lends itself to marvelous background settings of mountains and fjords, provides many varieties of plot — spying, sabotage, smuggling, hiding, escape, and rescue — all the trappings that children too often associate with war.

Benchley	**Bright Candles**
Bernhardsen	**Fight in the Mountains**
Bishop	**Twenty and Ten**
Cowan	**Children of the Resistance**
Levin	**Star of Danger**
McKown	**Patriot of the Underground**
McSwigan	**Snow Treasure**
Shemin	**The Empty Moat**
Van Stockum	**The Winged Watchman**
Wuorio	**Code: Polonaise**
Wuorio	**To Fight in Silence**

Appendix C

The Legacy of the Holocaust
A Supplementary Reading List

... these ashes would be indestructible and immutable, they would not burn up into nothingness because they themselves were remnants of fire. They would not freeze, but simply mingle with the snow and ice, never dying under the sun's hot glare because there's nothing more to dry out of ashes. No one living would ever be able to escape them; these ashes would be contained in the milk that will be drunk by babies yet unborn and in the breasts their mothers offer them; the ashes will linger in the flowers which grow out of them and in the pollen with which they will be fertilized by bees; they will be in the depths of the earth too, where rotted woodlands transform themselves into coal, and in the heights of the heaven, where every human gaze, equipped with a telescope, encounters the invisible layers which envelop this wormy terrestrial apple of ours. These ashes will be contained in the breath and expression of every one of us and the next time anybody asks what the air he breathes is made of, he will have to think about these ashes; they will be contained in books which haven't yet been written and will be found in the remotest regions of the earth where no human foot has ever trod; no one will be able to get rid of them, for they will be the fond, nagging ashes of the dead who died in innocence.

Arnost Lustig   **A Prayer for Katerina Horovitzova.**

So this story will not finish with some tomb to be visited in memoriam. For the smoke that rises from crematoriums obeys physical laws like any other; the particles come together and disperse according to the wind that propels them. The only pilgrimage, estimable reader, would be to look with sadness at a stormy sky now and then.

Andre Schwarz-Bart   **The Last of the Just.**

Appendix C

The Suggested Reading list was confined to books about certain historical events; it was limited in time and place. The effects of the Holocaust itself had no such limitations; people all over the world were affected, then and for many years to come. The books on this supplemental list are but a small sample of the widespread and continuing reverberations of the Holocaust. Some of these stories are set at the time of the war or soon after; others occur many years later, up to and including the present day. All of the books on the student's list, and about half of those on the adult list, are fiction. The non-fiction books are examples of what could be a much longer list. As with the Suggested Reading list, the aim here is to present a selective, rather than a comprehensive, bibliography.

Children

Asher   **Daughters of the Law**
Beaufort Books, 1980
The story of the 13-year-old daughter of a survivor, whose mother was not able to talk to her child about her experiences.

Bezdekova   **They Called Me Leni**
Bobbs-Merrill, 1973
Soon after the war, a little German girl discovers that she is really Czechoslovakian, abducted by the Germans and adopted by a German family.

Degens   **Transport 7-41-R**
Viking, 1974
A 13-year-old girl, and an elderly couple who wish to die in their homeland, travel back to Germany after the war.

Forman   **My Enemy, My Brother**
Hawthorn, 1969 (paper, Scholastic)
A young survivor of the Holocaust struggles with the moral issue of taking up arms to fight for the state of Israel.

Gottschalk   **In Search of Coffee Mountains**
> Nelson, 1977
> The setting is a displaced persons camp where, even after the war is over, the struggle for survival still goes on.

Greene   **Summer of My German Soldier**
> Dial, 1973 (paper, Bantam)
> During the war, a young Jewish girl in the United States befriends a German prisoner of war.

Kerr   **Gentlehands**
> Harper & Row, 1978
> A teenage boy, living in today's world, discovers his grandfather is suspected of having been a member of the Nazi SS.

Levoy   **Alan & Naomi**
> Harper & Row, 1977
> A young Jewish boy in New York City, in 1944, learns the meaning of both hatred and friendship as he tries to help a refugee girl.

Tunis   **His Enemy, His Friend**
> Morrow, 1967
> A former German soldier returns twenty years later to a town in France where he served during the occupation.

Adult

Epstein, Helen   **Children of the Holocaust: Conversations With Sons and Daughters of Survivors**
> Putnam, 1979 (paper, Bantam)
> Ms. Epstein, herself a child of survivors, began this project as part of a personal need to resolve the issues created in her by her parents' past. Much of the book is autobiographical; she moves back and forth between her own story and those of others that she interviewed in Canada, Israel and the United States. Although those she interviewed shared the common bond of being the children of survivors, their reactions, and their parents' reactions, were frequently quite different.

Appendix C

Kanfer, Stefan   **The Eighth Sin**
Random House, 1978
The Nazis persecuted Gypsies as well as Jews; the main character in this magnificent novel is a gypsy who, as a child, survived the concentration camp, was adopted and brought to the United States, but lived the rest of his life in the shadow of his past.

Niezabitowska, Malgorzata   **Remnants: The Last Jews of Poland**   Photographs by Tomasz Tomaszewski
Friendly Press, 1986
A study, in text and photographs, of the 5,000 Jews remaining in Poland, this is a beautiful and moving account of the remnants of a lost culture.

Rabinowitz, Dorothy   **New Lives: Survivors of the Holocaust Living in America**
Knopf, 1976 (paper, Avon)
This is a mosaic based on interviews with survivors all over the country, as they talk about their experiences in the Nazi camps and how they rebuilt their lives after the liberation.

Rothschild, Sylvia, ed.   **Voices From the Holocaust**
New American Library, 1981
The foreword to this collection was written by Elie Wiesel; the selections are transcripts from tapes of people living in the United States who are Holocaust survivors. Their statements have been divided into three sections: life before the Holocaust, life during the Holocaust, and life in America.

Sachar, Abram L.   **The Redemption of the Unwanted**
Marek, 1982
This volume concentrates on the first decade after the Holocaust, and the fate of those who survived. In the author's words, "How did they get out of the cemetery that Europe had become?" He describes ninety-pound skeletons emerging from camps, evading the British and resisting the Arabs to establish their own sovereign state.

Stone, I.F.   **Underground to Palestine and Reflections Thirty Years Later**
Pantheon, 1978
I.F. Stone was the first journalist to accompany a group of Jewish refugees to Palestine after the war, and this is the story of that trip. It is also the story of many of the individual refugees. First published in 1946, the added section to this edition gives Stone's views on the rights of Palestinians in the current Arab/Israeli struggle.

Uhlman, Fred   **Reunion**
>Farrar, Straus & Giroux, 1977 (paper, Penguin)
>A friendship between two boys—one Jewish, one Aryan— in Germany, in the early days of the Third Reich, is described in retrospect as reflected on by the Jewish boy, now an adult and no longer in Germany.

Wallant, Edward   **The Pawnbroker**
>Harcourt Brace, 1961
>The novel tells a dramatic story and draws a vivid character sketch of a survivor who became a pawnbroker in Harlem, after having been a university professor in pre-war Poland.

Wiesel, Elie   **The Accident**
>Hill and Wang, 1962 (paper, Avon)
>A young man combats friends and doctors, fighting for the right to die rather than continue to live with the horrors of the past.

Wiesel, Elie   **Dawn**
>Hill and Wang, 1961 (paper, Avon)
>A young survivor, now living in occupied Palestine, shifts from victim to executioner as he is ordered to kill a British hostage.

Wiesenthal, Simon   **The Murderers Among Us**
>McGraw-Hill, 1967 (paper, Bantam)
>Joseph Wechsberg has written a profile of Simon Wiesenthal, the best known of all the Nazi-hunters, which is interspersed with Wiesenthal's personal memoirs.

Appendix D

Human Behavior

The purpose of this section is to provide some suggestions for teachers or students who would like to explore some of the moral issues raised in the study of the Holocaust. One of the basic issues raised is that of prejudice: to what extent would Hitler's "Final Solution" have succeeded if antisemitism had not already been deeply rooted in the society of Germany and Eastern Europe? What is prejudice, and who are its victims? Is it always directed against those who have a different racial or ethnic background, or is it sometimes enough just to be different in some way from those around you? What is it like to be a victimizer, and why does it happen? Is it simply a matter of building yourself up by putting others down, or is it more complex than that? How strong and how deeply ingrained is a human being's capacity to inflict pain on another human being? Are we all capable of such behavior, or is it a moral flaw present only in some of us? There are many such questions, and few simple answers; the books listed here may not provide any answers, but they will help the reader to address the questions.

The books listed on the following pages are all written for young people. Adults will find the life and writing of Jack Henry Abbott to be a fascinating and disturbing study in human behavior. Abbott was 37 when he wrote **In the Belly of the Beast** (Random, 1981). He wrote the book while serving a prison term; from the age of twelve until the time the book was published, he had been incarcerated for all but nine and a half months. The book was compiled from a series of letters written by Abbott to Norman Mailer; it is a brilliant, powerful, and frightening look at Abbott himself and at our prison system. Mailer, together with Abbott's literary agent and his editor at Random House helped secure his parole in the early summer of 1981. A few weeks later, on the day that Terrence Des Pres' review of the book appeared in the New York Times Book Review (July 19, 1981), police were looking for Abbott in connection with the murder of a New York waiter. On September 20, 1981, a follow-up article appeared on the front page of the New York Times Book Review; this article discussed the reaction of the literary world to Abbott, quoting extensively from Jerzy Kosinski, another writer who had become involved with Abbott. Later that month, Abbott was captured in Louisiana; he was found guilty of manslaughter, and is now serving fifteen years to life. His second book, **My Return**, was published in 1987 (Prometheus Books).

American History

Slavery in America

There are many books available on slavery, but one of the best is **To Be a Slave**, by Julius Lester (Dial, 1968). It is a collection of memoirs of ex-slaves skillfully woven together to reveal both the way of life and the inner feelings of the slave. For a more detailed list of materials in this area, contact Facing History for the Middle Passage Bibliography.

Native Americans

Again, there are a number of books available, but a personal favorite is a novel, **The Year of the Three-Legged Deer**, by Eth Clifford (Houghton Mifflin, 1971). It is based on an actual event in history, also the subject of an adult novel, **The Massacre at Fall Creek**, by Jessamyn West; it depicts the massacre of a friendly band of Indians and the first time in American history that a white man was actually put on trial for killing an Indian.

The Japanese Internment Camps

Because relatively little material has been written for children on this subject, a more complete annotated list is included:

Conrat   **Executive Order 9066: The Internment of 110,000 Japanese Americans**
California Historical Society, 1972
Executive Order 9066 was the order signed by President Roosevelt on February 19, 1942, which authorized the Secretary of War to remove Japanese-Americans from their homes on the West Coast. This book is a moving photographic essay which documents that action.

Houston, Jeanne   **Farewell to Manzanar**
Houghton Mifflin, 1973 (paper, Bantam)
Jeanne Houston's maiden name was Wakatsuki, and this is the story of her childhood at Manzanar, an internment camp in California. Unlike the other books on this subject, Mrs. Houston continues her story to demonstrate the effect this internment had on their lives after they were allowed to return home. This is not actually a children's book, but the reading is not difficult.

Ishigo, Estelle   **Lone Heart Mountain**
Los Angeles: Japanese-American Citizens League, 1972
Estelle Ishigo was an American artist married to a Japanese-American and, at her request, interned with him at Lone Heart Mountain, Wyoming. This book and the sketches that illustrate it were written at that time, describing her life there and the lives of those around her.

Means, Florence Crannell   **The Moved-Outers**
Houghton Mifflin, 1945
This was the first book written for young people about the internmnment camps; it is a slightly old-fashioned, romanticized teenage novel, but the fact that it was written at all, in 1945, earns it a place on the shelves.

Takashima, Shizuye   **A Child in Prison Camp**
Tundra Books, 1971
The child and the camp in this book are both Canadian, but otherwise the story is similar to those by Houston and Ishigo. It is retold in diary form, and illustrated by Shizuye Takashima's paintings. Like Estelle Ishigo, she is an artist, and like Jeanne Wakatsuki, she spent her childhood years in an internment camp.

Uchida, Yoshiko   **Journey to Topaz**
Scribner, 1971
Like the Means book, this is fiction, but the child is younger. The author bases her story on fact, however, as she and her family were among those incarcerated in the Relocation Center in Topaz, Utah.

America Today

The United States has many minorities, but few of them are well represented in children's literature. One exception is the black American; a number of fine black writers have been writing children's books in the last decade or so. Virginia Hamilton and Sharon Bell Mathis are among the best in this category. Ms. Mathis's sensitive portrayal of a young black girl in **Listen for the Fig Tree** is an example, as is Ms. Hamilton's equally masterful characterization of a girl with mixed black and Indian heritage in **Arilla Sundown**.

There are also books about black Americans written by white authors, especially addressing black/white issues, as in John Neufeld's **Edgar Allen**, the story of a white family who adopts a black child. Child psychologist Robert Coles has written two books about school desegregation, **Dead End School** and **Saving**

Face; the first is told from the viewpoint of a black child bused into a white neighborhood, and the child in the second is the son of a white policeman attending a newly integrated school.

Human Differences

The titles listed below are all about young people who find themselves out of the mainstream simply because they are different in some way from those around them.

Guy, Rosa   **The Friends**
              Holt, Rinehart & Winston, 1973
       A young West Indian girl tries to overcome her aversion to her friend's extreme poverty.

Hall, Lynn   **Sticks and Stones**
              Follett, 1972 (paper, Dell)
              A boy's life is destroyed by gossip which accuses him of homosexuality.

Hamilton, Virginia   **The Planet of Junior Brown**
              Macmillan, 1971
       An overweight, overprotected prodigy and a homeless child of the streets try to help each other survive.

Holman, Felice   **Slake's Limbo**
Scribner, 1974
              A disturbed boy finds a refuge by living in a New York City subway.

Platt, Kin   **Hey Dummy**
              Chilton, 1971 (paper, Dell)
       The taunting of peers and the outrage of parents threaten Alan's friendship with a mentally retarded boy.

Samuels, Gertrude   **Adam's Daughter**
              Crowell, 1977
       A teenage girl enters the shaky world of the ex-con as she leaves family and friends to help her father readjust.

107

Conformity and Cruelty

The books in this category are not pleasant to read. They are in the **Lord of the Flies** genre, and raise many of the same issues. They all deal with young people who inflict pain on others, sometimes deliberately, sometimes thoughtlessly. What separates the victims from the victimizers, and what motivates the latter? How far will a group follow its leader when the game turns serious, and how does an individual break away?

Butler, William   **The Butterfly Revolution**
Ballantine (paper)
A group of boys at a summer camp stage a revolution.

Cormier, Robert   **The Chocolate War**
Pantheon, 1974
One boy tries to hold out against a gang that terrorizes a Catholic boy's school.

Crawford, Charles   **Bad Fall**
Harper & Row, 1972
A lonely boy becomes friends with a tough leader, whose "dirty tricks" soon become more than a game.

Degens, T.   **Game on Thatcher Island**
Viking, 1977
An 11-year-old boy is lured into joining a "war game" which ends in terror.

Duncan, David Douglas   **Killing Mr. Griffin**
Little Brown, 1978
A group of high schoolers try to disclaim responsibility when an attempt to frighten a teacher results in his death.

Fox, Paula   **How Many Miles to Babylon?**
White, 1967
Three older boys kidnap a 10-year-old runaway, to use him in their dog-stealing racket.

Zindel, Paul   **The Pigman**
Harper & Row, 1968
A lonely teenage couple make friends with an old man, and then get caught up in circumstances that nearly destroy his home.

Appendix E

Genocide of the Cambodian People

Becker, Elizabeth   **When the War Was Over**
Simon & Schuster, 1986
The most complete and accessible account of the history of the Cambodian Genocide. As a journalist who has covered Cambodian events since the 1960s, Becker uses extensive interviews and documentary evidence to explain the rise and fall of the Khmer Rouge. The book emphasizes the cultural and political roots to the genocide with a reportorial immediacy that grips the reader.

Chanda, Nayan   **Brother Enemy**
Harcourt, Brace, Jovanovich, 1986
This book focuses on the diplomatic machinations between Cambodia, Vietnam, China, the Soviet Union, and the United States after the Indochina War. Chanda uses his journalistic skills to weave together hundreds of interviews with the key players in the continuing conflict in Southeast Asia. Most valuable for a frank, behind-the-scenes look at regional politics.

May, Someth   **Cambodian Witness**
Random House, 1986
An autobiographical memoir of a young person's survival of the Cambodian Genocide. This firsthand testimony gives the reader an invaluable human dimension to the country's travails.

Ponchaud, Francois   **Cambodia: Year Zero**
Holt, Rinehart & Winston, 1977
While this book is dated and only covers the first year of the Khmer Rouge takeover, it is a very readable account by a firsthand observer of the fall of Phnom Penh. Ponchaud was a French missionary in Cambodia from 1965 to May 1975. This was one of the first authentic accounts of the genocide to reach the western world.

Szymusiak, Moyda   **The Stones Cry Out**
Hill & Wang, 1986
This is another powerful testimony of a young person who survived the Cambodian Genocide. Its stark and bleak tone brings the reader into the grinding misery of everyday life during those years.

Index

Holocaust and Human Behavior Bibliography

Index

113

Index

Holocaust and Human Behavior Bibliography

115

Index

Holocaust and Human Behavior Bibliography

117

Index

Holocaust and Human Behavior Bibliography

119

Index

Holocaust and Human Behavior Bibliography

Index

Holocaust and Human Behavior Bibliography

Index